Foreword
by the Hon. Lord MacLean

George Saunders spent his professional life as a journalist reporting court actions of all kinds, both civil and criminal. In this book he has made a fascinating collection of ten trials, all of which he attended, notebook in hand. Except for Carole Compton, who was tried in Italy, all the accused appeared before Scottish Courts and, principally, the High Court of Justiciary.

The strange, unusual, exceptional or bizarre in each is what links all ten trials. The trials themselves are, as one would expect from a writer of George Saunders' skill and experience, both accurately and grippingly recounted.

Having been engaged as counsel for the prosecution in two of the trials I can provide ample confirmation of that. Since it was reading about famous trials when I was a young schoolboy that prompted my early ambition to become an advocate if I could, I hope that others may have a similar experience in reading this book. I can thoroughly commend it to readers of all generations.

Edinburgh, 1991   Ranald MacLean

To my wife, Margaret,
with love for her
unstinting help and patience

Casebook of the Bizarre

A Review of Famous Scottish Trials

GEORGE SAUNDERS

Foreword by the Hon. Lord MacLean

JOHN DONALD PUBLISHERS LTD
EDINBURGH

© George Saunders 1991

All rights reserved. No part of this publication may
be reproduced in any form or by any means without
the prior permission of the publishers,
John Donald Publishers Ltd,
138 St Stephen Street, Edinburgh EH3 5AA.

ISBN 0 85976 353 6

British Library Cataloguing in Publication Data
A catalogue record for this book is available from
the British Library.

Phototypeset by Newtext Composition Ltd, Glasgow.
Printed & bound in Great Britain by Scotprint Ltd., Musselburgh.

Preface

Bizarre has many meanings, but the commonest of these is 'odd', 'fantastic' or 'extravagant'. In this volume of mainly Scottish trials, all the cases have something of a bizarre element, some funny, others horrifying, and still others just plain queer or strange.

I have chosen, after a lifetime spent in our law courts, some of Scotland's most famous or infamous trials, tackling them from a reporter's viewpoint of the legal process. Fortunately in Scotland we do not have opening speeches to the jury, as in England, and there is no opportunity of 'poisoning' the minds of jurors by statements by the Crown which they never prove conclusively by evidence.

That is why, when a jury reaches a verdict, it is seldom overturned on appeal; we therefore have not had the huge number of miscarriages of justice encountered in England in recent years.

Only one of the ten selected cases in this book was successful on appeal, and that was because of a judge's error and was not the fault of the jury.

Because of our remarkable 110-day rule, which means that anyone in custody must be brought to trial within 110 days, we have a sure and swift form of justice which is the envy of many other countries such as Italy, where, under the infamous Fascist Rocca Code, a person can be held in custody for up to four years before trial as a terrorist. Our system of corroboration also ensures that facts have to be proved by either a second witness verifying what the first witness testified or by surrounding facts and circumstances.

Scots law is able to hold its own and has also contributed widely to other systems of law. We were the first to change the punishment of juvenile offenders to a unique treatment-orientated system, and we also introduced legislation to combat alcohol abuse and crowd violence at sports meetings. We have for centuries had a system of public prosecutors, and this has now been copied in England, where the odious practice of prosecution by the police, has at long last been abandoned.

Although we now have a Contempt of Court Act, 1981, which covers the whole of the UK, judges in Scotland still tend to take a much stricter view of pre-trial publicity than they do in England, and this has led to many newspapers being fined heavily for contempt of court.

The criminal law is uncodified, and apart from offences created by statute, it is mainly contained in the common law. Our system of public prosecution is headed by the Lord Advocate, and apart from those bodies who are allowed to prosecute, private prosecution is practically unknown. All serious crimes are reported to the Crown Office, and the Lord Advocate and his staff direct whether and in what court the prosecution will take place. There is no such thing as an inquiry before an examining magistrate as there is under the inquisitorial system of law in Europe.

In Scotland there are three possible verdicts: Guilty, Not Guilty and the controversial Not Proven. The latter two result in the accused being liberated, and he is free from further prosecution on the same charge. The Not Proven verdict usually indicates grave suspicion, but the evidence is normally insufficient to convict.

The legal structure and system of law in Scotland are very different from England and Wales. The existence of Scots law was guaranteed by the Treaty of Union in 1707, but during the last 280 years the laws of both countries have been drawn closer together. A great deal of legislation now applies to the United Kingdom, including taxation, commerce, road traffic and many other large fields of law.

Unlike English law, Scots law has long been a systematized body of principles. The historical differences produced different kinds of legal systems, rules and institutions and also a different outlook and approach. It is often claimed that our system produces law which is more rational, coherent and systematic.

The judiciary are independent and free from interference by the Executive, but a judge can be removed from office should he become involved in politics. In 1978 a sheriff was removed by Parliament because of his involvement with the Scottish Plebiscite Society. In Scotland far greater use is made of full-time legally qualified judges than in England, where lay magistrates play a greater role. Unlike many European countries, our professional judges are drawn from legal practitioners, rather than from people specially trained in a judicial career structure.

Our criminal law is still essentially home-bred and has not been affected materially by English case law or legislation. Much of it is based on common law, whereas in England there has been a great deal of codification. As in England, we use the adversary system — the State versus the alleged offender — and not the inquisitorial system, as in most European countries.

The rules of procedure are very different in Scotland. We have a completely separate system of courts, different pre-trial procedure, a jury of 15 as opposed to only 12 in England, and different rules of evidence.

When the jury of 15 is selected both the prosecution and the defence may challenge the selection of up to three jurors without giving reasons, but there is no vetting of juries as there is in America. The prosecution must prove the case 'beyond reasonable doubt' and the law presumes the accused 'innocent until proved guilty'. There is no obligation for an accused to give evidence.

The High Court is in Parliament House in Edinburgh, but it also goes on circuit to other cities and to the principal towns in Scotland. The court deals with the most serious cases and is the only court able to try cases of treason, murder, attempted murder, rape and incest.

Prosecutions can be conducted by the Lord Advocate or the Solicitor General, but normally by Crown Counsel (or Advocates Depute as they are called).

Important points of law in criminal appeals can be heard by more than three judges. In 1977, seven judges reviewed the law relating to crimes committed while under the voluntary influence of drink or drugs, and they upheld the conviction of a youth who took LSD and 25 pints of lager before he murdered his father.

The ten cases I have chosen represent the most fascinating aspects of our legal system in operation in the present day. All of them are bizarre in one way or another.

Edinburgh, 1991   G.S.

Contents

CHAPTER 1

Bride's Unlucky Day

Eighteen-year-old Helga Konrad, farmer's daughter from the mountain village of Schwerbach 50 miles from Frankfurt, Germany, was a pleasant young teenager. No extrovert, she was a little withdrawn and shy until she suddenly fell madly in love.

Helga had left school at 15, going to domestic college for a year to be trained in cooking and housekeeping. After leaving college, she helped her father, Helmut Konrad, run the family farm. Like many German girls, she had studied English to an advanced level. She liked to give her pets English names, calling her dachshund "Rowdy" and her golden hamster "Teeny". She loved reading romances with an English flavour.

Coming from a rural background, Helga was chaperoned everywhere she went. She had a daily round of feeding the cows and pigs on the farm but the constant attendance of her father when she went to a dance or to night classes left her ill-prepared for the big world outside. She proved easy prey for the self-confident young suitor who suddenly came into her life.

Helga's life changed dramatically the day she replied to an advertisement placed in the lonely hearts column of a local newspaper by a well-dressed, smooth, 21-year-old Dutchman named Ernst Dumoulin. It was just after her 18th birthday in June, 1972 that Helga met Ernst and fell in love. She later introduced him to her father but never explained how they had met. Dumoulin seemed keen to marry Helga but her father thought she was too young and that she had not had enough time to get to know her boyfriend properly.

Herr Konrad did not quite trust Dumoulin. He thought he was cool and calculating and when, on his second visit to the farm, the young Dutchman told him, 'We want to marry,' Helga's father replied, 'One doesn't marry that quickly.'

'I tried very hard to postpone their wedding plans until I established that he would be in a position to support a wife,'

Konrad would later explain. He was chairman of the supervisory board of the local branch of his bank and Dumoulin coolly asked him to get him a job there. But Konrad told him this was 'absolutely out of the question', feeling it would be unethical to employ someone who might become his son-in-law.

Konrad's efforts to delay the proposed wedding were doomed to failure. He tried to persuade the couple to wait until Christmas and then sent Helga with a friend to Lake Garda in Italy for a holiday. Trying to buy time for his only daughter, he also told them if they waited until the spring to marry he would give them, 15,000 marks as starting capital. But even that was not enough for the ambitious Dumoulin, who was in a hurry to break into the financial world.

Although Dumoulin was born in Minden, Germany, he was a Dutch national. Between 1966 and 1969 he studied banking and worked as a trainee bank assistant, only to leave the bank before the end of his three-month probationary period. Later, it was found he owed the bank a loan of £600 and that his current account was overdrawn by £260. He became engaged in 1971, but the arrangement was broken off a month later. On 24 June 1972, he advertised for a pen-friend in the lonely hearts column of the Koblenz *Rhein Zeitung*: 'Young man (21) seeks for missing opportunity, a nice girl with a view to marriage later'. Fatefully, Helga Konrad replied.

Dumoulin soon convinced the naive young girl that they should elope. He traded in his car and wrote a cheque for a new one, knowing that he did not have the money to cover it in his bank account.

On 15 September 1972, Dumoulin arrived at the Konrad farm in a new red Fiat sports car and Helga asked her father's permission to go for a spin. That night, Helga failed to return. Her parents discovered that a travelling bag and clothes were missing from her room; they reported her disappearance to the police.

After Helga eloped, the Konrads heard nothing until October 10, when the son of a neighbouring farmer came across the fields to tell them Helga had phoned to wish her father a happy birthday and to tell him she would be home the following Sunday.

But when Sunday came, a specially-baked 'Welcome Home' cake ready for Helga's return, the only news that the Konrads received of their daughter was of her tragic death two days earlier.

The young couple had arrived in London from Paris making a connection to Edinburgh on September 19. On the Edinburgh flight they met civil servant Duncan Clark, a 52-year-old higher executive officer at the Civil Service College in Edinburgh. They asked Mr Clark how they could get from Edinburgh to Newcastle, thinking they could then carry on to Gretna Green. They explained that they wanted to get married.

When the plane landed in Edinburgh, Clark took the couple to his college bar. One of the students they met there volunteered to take them to a boarding house.

Before leaving, Ernst and Helga asked Clark about the residential qualifications for getting married in Scotland. Clark advised Helga to tell her parents where they were, but Dumoulin said: 'We do not want to go back to Germany ever.' Herbert Wood, who ran a boarding house in Torphichen Street, gave the couple his only available accommodation, a large room with two beds, for which they paid in advance for two weeks. Mr Wood and his wife acted as their witnesses at Haymarket registry office on the fateful Friday the 13th of October.

The couple had also invited Mr Clark and a friend. After the ceremony they all went to a bar for drinks to celebrate. Mr Wood paid for a wedding breakfast in a restaurant and left the Dumoulins there. They later returned to the boarding house and an hour later went out again. The boarding house owner would never see Helga again, for some hours later she plunged 100 feet to her death from the top of Edinburgh's famous Salisbury Crags.

A couple from Coldstream were driving through Holyrood Park about 9 p.m. after visiting their daughter nearby when a young man, in a distressed condition, ran towards their car shouting: 'Ambulance, ambulance. My wife has fallen.' The couple drove back to their daughter's home to dial 999, returning with their daughter, a blanket, a torch and a towel. They could not find Dumoulin. Then, half an hour later, they saw a man being helped into a car.

A motorist who had stopped in the Park, John Munro, said Dumoulin staggered across to his car and said, 'Accident. Accident. My wife has fell.' Dumoulin was hysterical, screaming and banging on the roof and windows of his car. The police arrived and took him into their car. When he asked him how serious the accident was, Dumoulin said, 'I left her for dead.'

'If he was acting he must have been very good. He was really hysterical,' Munro told the court.

Afterwards the police discovered that Helga's husband of only a few hours had taken out £412,000 insurance on her life in the event of an accident. When he was searched by the police, he only had 14½ pence in his possession.

Thus it was that exactly one month after his daughter's elopement, Herr Konrad received a telephone call from Dumoulin in Scotland.

Konrad asked where his daughter was.

Dumoulin said, 'We are married.'

When Konrad asked to speak to Helga, Dumoulin replied, 'Helga is in Heaven,' adding 'Helga is dead . . . an accident.'

The father said later, 'I shall never forget the words as long as I live.' He said Dumoulin even asked him, 'May I now, since I became your son-in-law, address you as "Du"?' which is a word in German when you are very familiar. When Konrad asked where he was telephoning from, Dumoulin answered, 'Edinburgh, Scotland. Torphichen Street, No 9.'

Although Herr Konrad caught a flight to Scotland immediately he did not really believe his daughter was dead, and suspected that Dumoulin might be trying to blackmail him. But, on his arrival, the tragic news of his daughter's 'accident' was soon confirmed by the police.

The next day, Konrad confronted Dumoulin across a table at police headquarters in Edinburgh, 'Be honest', he told him, 'once in your lifetime.' Dumoulin maintained that Helga's death was accidental – that she had 'fallen down a mountain.' To the incredulous father he explained that they had gone on their wedding day to see Salisbury Crags and returned later that evening to see the lights of the city. Dumoulin claimed that he had turned his back to his young bride for a moment when he heard a cry. He turned around again, to find that she had disappeared.

Neither Herr Konrad nor the police were satisfied with Dumoulin's explanation. When further investigation revealed that he had taken out heavy insurance on the life of his young bride in the event of an accident, Dumoulin was charged with her murder.

Herr Konrad returned to Germany to arrange his daughter's funeral. There, he received a curious letter from Dumoulin:

Dear Family Konrad
This letter you will see I am sending from prison. I sit here being accused of having murdered my wife, Helga. Because Helga was your only child, her death must have hit you terribly, terribly hard.

Up to now my life has been full of misfortune but I still intended only the best. I would now like to express my sincere sympathy to you on the tragic death of your daughter. I must also emphasise that, at all times, I considered Helga my wife. Your wish never to see me again I accept. I am not a murderer . . .
Ernst Dumoulin, Edinburgh, 15th October 1972

Dumoulin's trial began in the High Court in Edinburgh on Tuesday, 23 January 1973 before a jury of eight women and seven men.

Fresh-faced and dapper, sporting metal-framed spectacles, Dumoulin kept glancing round the crowded courtroom, where his parents and the parents of his bride sat in the public benches.

The indictment accused him of 'forming a criminal purpose' in taking out insurance on the life of another, whose death he intended to procure.

It was alleged that Dumoulin had obtained a car in Germany by false pretences and, having sold it again, lodged part of the proceeds (£250) in the Bank of Nova Scotia in Princes Street, Edinburgh. It was further alleged that between September 20 and 30, he pretended to the bank manager that he had interests in Germany from which he could transfer funds or securities to the value of £10,000 for lodging of security against a loan of the same amount. According to the indictment, Dumoulin in fact had no transferrable interests in Germany; he had thus attempted to defraud the bank.

It was also alleged that Dumoulin induced Helga to complete four application forms to Hambro Life Assurance on

September 28 for sums totalling £206,184 in the event of her natural death and £412,368 in the event of her accidental death. He used the money he had deposited at the bank of Nova Scotia to pay the initial premium.

Finally, Dumoulin was accused of murdering Helga Konrad by pushing her over Salisbury Crags, with intent to obtain money by fraud, in pursuance of his criminal purpose.

The trial was conducted by Lord Wheatley, Lord Justice Clerk, with Mr James Milligan, QC (now Lord Milligan) for the Crown and Mr Frederick O'Brien, QC later to become Sir Frederick O'Brien, Sheriff Principal of Lothian and the Borders) for the defence. Because of Dumoulin's limited English, an interpreter was used throughout the trial. Dumoulin pleaded not guilty and submitted a special plea of self defence, alleging that he was assaulted by his wife.

The dead bride's heartbroken father was one of the first witnesses. He told the court that when Dumoulin called at the farm in his new red sports car, Helga said she would only be away 15 minutes. But he never saw her alive again.

Asked what sort of mood Dumoulin was in when he telephoned with the terrible news of his daughter's death, Herr Konrad said, 'I did at one time detect a sort of sigh – maybe tears – over the phone, but he is such a wonderful actor I cannot say.' Konrad further testified that in a second phone call later that day, Dumoulin sounded quite normal and was able to spell out Torphichen Street to him.

Dumoulin, sitting in the dock between two policemen, listened intently to the translation of the evidence. Occasionally he glanced over at the exhibits of his wife's blood-stained clothing and at the sleeve of a soundtrack recording from the film *Love Story*.

The boarding house keeper, Mr Wood, testified that in the early hours of the morning after his wedding, Dumoulin arrived with two detectives. They told him Helga was dead. Dumoulin, who normally was smartly dressed had bandages on his arm and was covered in mud.

Later, Wood stated, he went into Dumoulin's room to turn off the gas. Dumoulin appeared to be dazed and upset. Wood feared that he might gas himself. The following day, after visiting the police station, Dumoulin returned to the boarding house and asked if he could use the record player. He wanted to play his *Love Story* record. Wood added 'It was obviously a record that had sentimental connections with Dumoulin and his wife. They brought about 11 records with them. We heard them play this one more than any other.'

Helga, Wood testified, spoke quite good English. He had gathered that she was going to be her husband's secretary and that Dumoulin was going to open up a business as a financial adviser.

Dumoulin's father, Geradus Dumoulin, a 50-year-old welfare worker from Meinefield, West Germany, testified that Ernst was the youngest of three sons. In 1972 Ernst left home to work in a bank 250 miles away. Herr Dumoulin never met Helga and his son never told him how she came to die. Ernst's only asset was his salary.

Dumoulin's bank manager in West Germany, Heinz Gantze, testified that after two months the bank was not satisfied with his work. Dumoulin left, owing the bank 4,561 Deutschmarks in relation to a loan of 5,000 DM and overdrawn by 2,000 DM.

The court was also told that the young couple opened a bank account with the Bank of Nova Scotia in Edinburgh on September 20, depositing £250 in their joint names. Two days later they withdrew £50 and, on September 28 a further £199, leaving a balance of only £1.

The relief manager of the bank stated that the couple walked in off the street and asked for a loan of £10,000. Dumoulin said he had £10,000 or the equivalent in a German bank which he could transfer as collateral. The relief manager told Dumoulin he would need a banker's reference. Helga, who had a better understanding of English, sat with her German-English dictionary but took no part in the conversation. Dumoulin's attitude towards the girl appeared to be 'formal' considering the fact they were to be married.

A life insurance inspector with Scottish Life Assurance described for the court how, three days after their arrival in Edinburgh, Dumoulin and Helga came to his office and asked for policies worth £200,000 on the lives of both of them. The company did not proceed with the policies, which would have required monthly premiums of between £350 and £400.

Insurance salesman William Syer of Hambro testified that he

met the couple in the Caledonian Hotel, Edinburgh, on September 28 to discuss policies they wanted to take out. Dumoulin told him he wanted to spend £400 a month on insurance for himself and his wife.

Mr Syer informed the couple that this would mean four policies on the life of each of them for cover of £200,000. This worked out at cover of £206,184 on the life of Helga and £412,368 in the event of her accidental death and £190,480 on Dumoulin's life – double for accidental death. Monthly premiums would amount to £443. Dumoulin said he would be able to pay this from assets he had in Germany, which would be sent to him on the 16th of the month. Syer stated:

> When we went over the brochure together he was especially interested in the sickness and accident protection. He wanted to know if the policy covered accidental death and said he wanted extra cover for accidental death. He said he did not want cover until after the wedding.

When asked for a month's premium in advance, Dumoulin explained he would not have the full amount until the 16th of the month but could pay half immediately. He took Mr Syer to the Bank of Nova Scotia, where he withdrew money, giving him £221.85.

Syer explained to Dumoulin that this would mean that only half of the policies would come into force initially. Four of the policies, two each for husband and wife, would operate from October 1 and four from November 1. However, since the proposals were never completed, the policies were never processed.

Asked if his company was ever at risk, Mr Syer replied, 'I would say no.'

Pressed further on this point, he added: 'It is possible it could be argued in a court of law. To the best of my knowledge I don't think I can answer that question.'

Dumoulin met the insurance salesman in a city hotel on the Sunday after the tragedy and told him of Helga's death. He said they were in the park beside the palace and that she had fallen. Dumoulin then commented that the insurance company would not pay because she had been killed on a mountain. Mr

Syer took this to be a reference to a clause about hazardous pursuits.

Dumoulin told the salesman that the police had trusted him and let him go. They had not asked him about insurance and he had not raised the subject. He wanted to know if information about the insurance would be released. When Syer said it would, Dumoulin asked if it was not possible to tear up the forms. Dumoulin seemed to assume the policies were in force, although there was no question of them being active until October 16. It was not just an insurance policy, Mr Syer pointed out to the court, but an investment which could have paid out more than £1 million. He was satisfied that none of the policies had ever reached the stage of coming into force.

Mr Syer told the court that he was under a certain amount of stress and he did not want simply to say to Dumoulin, 'The policies are not valid. Go away.' He felt he should have taken more care to ensure the policies began on the day of the marriage but it was at Dumoulin's request that they were to become active three days after. He agreed that Dumoulin might have thought the policies were in force from the date of the wedding.

Dr John Hillsdon Smith, police surgeon and lecturer in forensic medicine at Edinburgh University, gave a graphic description of how Helga might have been pushed to her death. She had very severe head injuries, a fractured spine and broken ankles. Because of the type of shoes she was wearing and the nature of the ground at the top of the cliff, it was unlikely, in his opinion, that she had slipped and fallen. The doctor testified:

One possible sequence which would agree with the medical findings and the other findings on the ground would be that this girl went over the cliff feet first and landed on a protruding rock, breaking her ankles.

This rock acted, together with her ankles, as a springboard from which she was projected some distance out from the rock face. She fell vertically and landed head first.

The body became folded up and she slid the rest of the way down the bank, across the Radical Road, to end up where she was found.'

In Dr Smith's opinion, this scenario would be consistent with a push. Without hypothesising a push or propelling force, he could not envisage the same sequence of events. There was one other possibility – a suicidal leap. But persons deliberately propelling themselves from a cliff would not jump onto a rock 12 feet below. If Helga had simply slipped, she would have slithered down the rock face, in which case one would expect her injuries to have been different. Her fall did not appear to have resulted from a simple slip over the edge because of wet grass or poor adhesion.

Edinburgh's deputy police surgeon, Dr Robert Nagle, described for the court how he was lowered on a rope 100 feet down the cliff face to test the theory as to how Helga died. His findings were inconsistent with the girl simply having slipped or fallen over the edge. She had left the cliff face and descended in 'a kind of swallow dive' before striking the outcrop 28 feet below. Given the character of the rock face, Dr Nagle stated, if Helga had simply slipped, one would expect her to have suffered far greater number of superificial injuries and fractures.

William Thomson, a police constable in Edinburgh who spoke fluent German, had been called to headquarters to act as interpreter when Dumoulin was being questioned over his wife's death. Thomson told the court that when Dumoulin was charged with Helga's murder, he replied in German, 'I did push my wife so that she fell down the cliff. I did not intend to murder her or have the intent of gaining money. I am not a murderer.'

Asked if he wished to make a reply in English, Dumoulin said, 'I have pushed my wife so that she fell down. I am not a murderer. I did not do it as a murder.'

The accused husband, who had sat impassively throughout the trial, listening intently to the translation of the evidence, lost his composure while the policeman was being questioned. 'Liar'! he shouted loudly in German. Then he put his hand to his face, took off his glasses and wiped his eyes with a handkerchief.

Detective Chief Inspector Alistair Morrison, who led the investigation, testified that Dumoulin told him his wife might be expecting a baby. Describing the circumstances of Helga's death, he said they had been sitting on a stone. He got up and she said, 'Oh.' He turned and saw her fall. Dumoulin claimed that he thought she had slipped on a stone. He heard her scream and ran down to her. There was a pool of blood but he could do nothing. He ran back and stopped a car.

Dumoulin also stated that his wife was *not* insured, that his parents were divorced and that he did not know where they were living. After two insurance men brought the policy documents to the police station, Dumoulin was allowed a solicitor and was then charged with murder.

Martin McGregor, who was in Saughton Prison at the same time as Dumoulin, said the accused told him that he and his wife were 'winching' (courting) at the top of the cliff, looking down on the city. According to Dumoulin's description, they started to get up to leave. His wife rose first; there was something wrong with Dumoulin's ankle and, when he was half-way up, his wife tried to assault him. He grabbed her by the wrists and pushed her back. He turned away, then turned back and saw her falling.

Dumoulin also told McGregor about the insurance but said he would not receive any money. He gave him a document but McGregor didn't really understand it.

McGregor said he asked Dumoulin why his wife would try to assault him. Dumoulin said it was because he was insured, adding that his wife was insured as well. He would not get the money, he explained, because of his wife's signature or something.

Mr Milligan for the Crown asked McGregor, 'Did he ever indicate it was of importance for there to be a witness?' 'No.'

'Or that it was of importance to him to establish it was an accident?' 'No.'

The document mentioned in McGregor's testimony consisted partly of writing and partly of diagrams. It read:

October 13 Friday. The witness depend on a few minutes after 8 o'clock. He saw two young people. He sat down 15 yards behind the young couple and they kissed together for much time and did speak but the witness could not understand what was talking.

He stood up quickly and she slowly. With one step she was behind him and pushed him with both hands. She assault him with both hands.

He seize her by wrists and she was trying to push him over cliff. He pushed her away and she stumbled and fall down. Then he went away. After five or six yards he heard a cry from her. He run to cliff and call her name.

With the document was a drawing of a hill and a figure with an arrow pointing to it marked 'Wife.' The figure had its arms in the air.

Also on the document were the words, 'Part One – the essentials.' The document appeared to be a fly-leaf from a book. When the document was read in court, Dumoulin's mother broke down and had to leave court.

These documents, coupled with Dumoulin's replies to the charge of murder, were damning. It was obvious he had tried to enlist the other prisoner as a witness, writing the documents as a guideline to his latest story even though it conflicted with his earlier explanations. Dumoulin was obviously grasping at straws to find a convincing defence.

The Crown having concluded its case, Dumoulin himself was the only witness for the defence. Speaking in German through a young woman interpreter, he claimed that he and his wife had devised a plan to defraud insurance companies. On their second day in Edinburgh, Dumoulin told the court, they had been talking about the future. Then, as a joke, he said they could defraud an insurance company. Helga, however, thought this was a good idea.

The plan had never been perfected but the idea was for his life to be insured and for him to disappear so the police would presume he was dead. He was to leave some of his personal belongings in a ruin on Cramond Island in the river Forth near the city and to wound himself to leave traces of blood. Dumoulin explained:

After falling down, I was to swim back to the mainland and disappear like that. I believed if they found some of my possessions there, Helga would go to the police and tell them I was missing and, after some time, the police had to assume I was dead.

After this she could go to the insurance company to get the money. After that, we would have met somewhere, sometime.

They filled in the proposal forms, Dumoulin testified, but Helga had signed her name as Helga Dumoulin and not Konrad. He had taken a policy on Helga's life because when he pretended to have the accident the police could have got the idea that Helga had tried to get rid of him. After their wedding, they went to the Palace of Holyroodhouse, taking a walk in the park before returning to the boarding house.

They returned to the park later that evening and sat down near the edge of cliff. Before getting up to go back, Helga kissed him. She had never done this before. As they were getting up he felt his back being hit forcefully:

> I am sure God saved my life at that moment because I did not fall forward but my body folded. I turned my head towards Helga. She was standing behind me and I looked at her and she looked at me. She came towards me. I took her at the wrists and she tried to push me towards the edge. The only chance I saw was to get myself into a better position. I pulled Helga towards the cliff.
>
> I wanted to get her back to reason, to calm her down. I pushed her away. I can't say. She stumbled, turned then she fell, and went over. She fell head first.

At this point in Dumoulin's testimony, Helga's father, red-faced and angry, stormed out of court muttering oaths in German. He pushed his way along the crowded public benches and was led from the court by a policeman and a relative. His wife stayed behind, quietly weeping.

Dumoulin continued his testimony, describing how he ran down to his wife but could not do anything. Later he learned she was dead.

He told the court that when he met the insurance salesman two days later, he wanted to make it clear there was no question of an insurance claim as there had been no cover for mountaineering in the policy.

Under cross-examination by Mr Milligan, Dumoulin stated that he had £300 when he arrived in Edinburgh and that he had lied when he claimed he had £10,000 for security in Germany.

The plan to defraud the insurance companies, Dumoulin claimed, had been formulated before he applied to the Bank of Nova Scotia for a loan. The policies would have required £442 in monthly premiums – an amount he had no prospect of saving.

Before they went to the park for the second time on their wedding day, Dumoulin said, he and his bride had not argued at any time. He did not believe Helga wanted to kill him for money, but could only assume, as unlikely as it might seem, that she was insane at the moment of their struggle on the cliff.

Mr Milligan called for a reconstruction in court of what happened on the cliff top. With the court macer, Jimmy Turnbull, acting the part of Helga, Dumoulin stepped down from the witness box to demonstrate his version of events.

Mr Turnbull was told to raise his arms while Dumoulin grabbed his wrists, swivelled round and pushed him away two or three yards.

Dumoulin agreed his wife went over the cliff as a result of him pushing her. But when Mr Milligan accused him of murdering her, he shouted, 'You are a liar.' He denied making a plan to take out insurance with the intention of murdering his young bride.

Mr Milligan, addressing the jury, stated that Dumoulin was clearly a discontented and frustrated young man who had been keen for promotion and had wanted to make a lot of money when he was working for a bank in Germany. When the young couple came to Edinburgh, Dumoulin was overdrawn on his bank account and had still to pay off the loan for his car. His assets at best were £100–£130. He realised £330 by selling his car, which he had not even paid for.

The plan for Dumoulin to disappear on Cramond Island so that his bride could claim the insurance money was, Mr Milligan asserted 'too far-fetched to be acceptable.' Dumoulin had shown himself in evidence to be quick-witted and not so naive as to believe he could disappear in order to get insurance money. He had an opportunity on their first visit to the park to make a reconnaissance of the crags and brought Helga back that evening with the deliberate intention of pushing her over. 'Where better a place, where no one would see what happened, where death was very likely and where it would not be too difficult to make out an accident had occurred.'

On the evidence, Mr Milligan said, he was sure Helga was

innocent. Dumoulin had £5 in cash, £1 in his bank account, was overdrawn on his German bank account, was due payments for the car he had sold and was due to pay £221 insurance premiums on October 15.

'He found himself in a desperate situation that night on the crags.'

Helga, Mr Milligan continued, was 'a thoroughly pleasant, likeable girl' who had been led along by Dumoulin, a man with a real motive for disposing of her.

Mr O'Brien, for the defence, said that while a hare-brained plan to defraud an insurance company was one thing, murder, with all its horror, was quite another. It would be as cruel a blow as anyone could suffer for a young man to see his young wife topple to her death on their wedding day. It would be just and right for him to be charged with murder if he was guilty. 'But to be innocent of the murder and wrongly convicted and sentenced to imprisonment for life would surely be a nightmare worse than any tale of horror thought up by Edgar Allan Poe.'

Lord Wheatley, in his summing-up, said the jury might think the allegations against Dumoulin were more likely to be encountered in a fictional thriller than in a court of law. 'But although the case presented by the Crown contains some bizarre elements that does not mean necessarily that they are not true. Equally it does not mean that they are.'

The jury were out for just over two hours before returning a majority verdict of 'Guilty.' However, on the judge's direction, they returned a formal verdict of not guilty on the charge of attempting to defraud the Bank of Nova Scotia of £10,000. They also deleted from the indictment that the murder was carried out 'in pursuance of a criminal purpose' conceived in Germany when Dumoulin disposed of a car bought with a loan which had not been repaid and bought a new car with a dishonoured cheque.

Helga's parents were not in court to hear the verdict. At his home high above the Rhine valley, Herr Konrad said 'I just could not wait in Scotland for the end of the trial. It was all too upsetting for me and my wife. Nothing can bring back the life of my daughter but at least justice has been done.' He added that he could never sufficiently thank the Scottish people and the police for all their kindness during the terrible time.

Baby-faced Dumoulin showed little emotion as the sentence of life imprisonment was passed on him. Lord Wheatley explained to him that the sentence did not necessarily mean he would spend the rest of his life in prison; but could be released on licence after a number of years.

As he was being led out of court, Dumoulin's parents, sitting a few yards behind the dock, both broke into tears. Mrs Dumoulin shouted, 'Es ist nicht wahr' (It is not true) before she was led out of court by a policewoman. Meeting his parents in a side room, Ernst Dumoulin finally broke down and wept. And so ended the ambitions of a humble bank clerk who dreamed of the world of high finance.

But if Helga's grief-stricken father had had his way there would not have been any trial. The police would not allow him to be alone with Dumoulin at any time, for, as Herr Konrad explained bitterly, 'They thought if we were left alone together, I would try to kill him. They were right. That is what I would have done.'

Helga is buried only 300 yards away from her parents' farmhouse. Her grave is marked by a simple black cross with the inscription: 'Helga Konrad – 1972.'

CHAPTER 2
The Biter Bit

The science of forensic odontology was still in its infancy in March 1968 when Scottish legal history was made by the conviction of an 18-year-old approved schoolboy, Gordon Hay, known as 'Gags', for the murder of a 15-year-old Biggar schoolgirl, Linda Peacock. The successful use of odontology to identify Hay as the murderer by the bite mark he left on the young girl's breast was hailed as 'a forensic triumph.' Scottish courts had always been slow to accept the latest advances in science but, surprisingly, showed a new receptiveness on this occasion to careful scientific evidence in what became a classic case of circumstantial evidence.

Even the presiding judge, Lord Grant, the late Lord Justice Clerk of Scotland, described the case as 'unique, difficult and puzzling.'

The eminent pathologist, Professor Keith Simpson, then head of the Department of Forensic Medicine at Guy's Hospital, London, and leading expert on odontology, gave evidence at the trial. He had the highest praise for the Scottish team, who produced crucial evidence and showed infinite patience and attention to detail. They produced, he said, the finest 'bite mark' photography and dentition-matching that had yet been brought to court.

Both the Scottish experts, Detective-Inspector Osborne Butler and Dr Warren Harvey, who later became honorary consultant Forensic Odontologist to the Glasgow Police, were aware that their work on the case was vital. The only proof of the murderer's identity, their evidence survived a most searching cross-examination at the trial.

Linda Peacock, who was only 5ft 1in tall, was the youngest of eight children. She was a bright and lively girl, interested in ponies, records and, naturally at her age, boys. She spent the afternoon of Sunday, 6 August 1967 at a farm busy with her favourite pastime, exercising ponies.

Linda then spent the evening in the Lanarkshire market

17

town of Biggar. Normally, she would have gone to her sister's home in Main Street to wait for one of her brothers to take her home.

But, on that fateful evening, her sister was on holiday. Linda set off to walk more than a mile to her home at Swaire Cottage. She was last seen talking to friends in the town about 9.30pm. Next morning, she was found strangled under a yew tree in St Mary's Cemetery, only 269 yards away from where she was last seen alive. The police said there were sadistic touches to the murder and a massive manhunt began. The cemetery in unlit Carwood Road was screened from the narrow road by a 5-foot-high wall. It was not locked at night and was often used by courting couples.

The murder hunt was led by Detective Chief Superintendent William Muncie, the head of Lanarkshire CID who had successfully led investigations into 50 murders, including those committed by mass murderer, Peter Manuel. He later became Assistant Chief Constable of Strathclyde before his well-earned retirement. Muncie's patience, clever reasoning and dogged determination had made him a legend in the force.

More than 100 officers from the Lanarkshire force and the Regional Crime Squad began a house-to-house search in the vicinity immediately after Linda was found. Tracker dogs were used in the surrounding fields and every male over 14 in the area was interviewed. A young couple had been seen on the road near the cemetery at about 10.15 p.m., just after Linda, on her own, was seen by two men who knew her and waved to her as they drove home. A woman told the police she heard a scream coming from the cemetery late on the Sunday evening.

Police began compiling reports on the movements of inmates and ex-inmates of nearby Loaningdale Approved School. The small town itself was in the grip of fear lest the killer would strike again. A petition calling for the return of capital punishment was signed by 20,000 people.

Nine days after the crime, the police returned to the scene of the murder to comb the area inch - by - inch. The bereaved parents, George Peacock, a retired electrician, and his wife, Mary, made an impassioned plea to the public for information.

But the investigation into their daughter's death would prove to be a slow and painstaking forensic exercise, and Hay would not be arrested and charged with the murder until 110 days after the crime. The police interviewed more than 300 people, drawing up a short list of 29 who could possibly have been involved. All of the short-listed individuals agreed to dental impressions being taken. After these were compared with transparencies of the bite marks on the girl's breast, the list was reduced to five.

Second impressions were then taken of these five. Six weeks after the murder, the team of four dental experts told the authorities they had eliminated everyone on the list except for No 11. It was only at this stage that it was revealed to them, in confidence, that No 11 was in fact Gordon Hay.

A further impression was still required in order for the dental experts to be absolutely certain. The Crown then took the unique step of applying to Sheriff-Substitute Gordon Gillies, QC at Lanark for a warrant to authorise a third impression of Hay's teeth. The warrant was granted.

Hay, by then, was the principal suspect but had not yet been arrested. For this reason, the legality of taking a third impression of his teeth would be fiercely contested at his trial.

Largely on the strength of the odontological evidence, Hay was charged with the murder of Linda Peacock. Appearing at a pleading diet at Lanark, he lodged a special defence of alibi. When his trial opened in the High Court in Edinburgh on Monday, 26 February 1968, before a jury of six women and nine men, the Crown listed 105 witnesses, including Professor Simpson and other dental and medical experts.

Hay pleaded not guilty to murdering Linda by striking her on the head with an instrument, biting her on the breast, tying a ligature round her wrist and her neck and strangling her. His special defence of alibi claimed that between 9 p.m. and midnight, when the crime was alleged to have been committed, he was in the approved school.

Prosecuting for the Crown was Mr Ewan Stewart, QC, then Solicitor-General for Scotland who had already established a reputation as a terrier of a prosecutor – probably the best prosecutor in Scotland for many years. His patient and sometimes aggressive cross-examinations had proved the downfall of many criminals. He was assisted by Mr Hugh Morton (now Lord Morton of Shuna, a judge in the Court of

Session). For the defence there was an equally tenacious Stewart, Mr Ian Stewart, QC (now Lord Allanbridge), who was assisted by Mr James Law. Their battle over the medical evidence was to prove the highlight of the trial.

Lord Grant immediately ruled that no witnesses under 17 should be named, adding that inmates of the approved school who were over 17 should be treated in the same way.

Five local girls, all aged 15 or 16, told the court that girls had dates with boys from the school and that a pre-arranged signal – an owl hoot – was used to attract the attention of the boys when they were not meant to be out of the school. The boys, they said, got out of the school through the gymnasium.

One girl said Linda had a boyfriend in the school but he had left. Another girl recalled Linda speaking to Hay and another boy on Saturday, 5 August 1967 – the day before she was murdered – at a fun fair at Biggar.

The girls all said the boys at the school could come and go as they pleased, especially at weekends. One girl said she met boys from the school at the pictures on Saturday nights and went to dances at the school.

A 16-year-old boy who was a pupil at the school at the time said he was with Hay when they met Linda at the fun fair. Linda spoke to the boy but he walked on. Hay stayed behind, but his schoolmate did not know if he said anything to Linda. Afterwards, however, Hay told him he would not mind a night with her. Hay's schoolmate also described how some of the boys from the school had attended a camp at Montrose. After a beach barbecue on Friday, 4 August, the night before they returned, he saw one of the boys pick up a metal hook on the beach. On the evening of Linda's murder, at about 9 p.m. he saw Hay wearing pyjamas, a dressing gown and boots in his dormitory. He did not see Hay again that night.

But a 15-year-old boy who was also a pupil at the time said that when, after the murder, the police arrived at the school, Hay told him something like, 'We were in the dorm all last night'. He understood that this was what he was to tell the police, although it was not true.

Mr Ewan Stewart asked, 'Were you invited by Hay to tell a lie?' The boy replied, 'That was what it sounded like but I wasn't sure.'

The boy remembered Hay going to the toilet in his pyjamas. Afterwards he fell asleep and woke up with the wireless playing. He did not know how long he had been asleep.

Cross-examined by Mr Ian Stewart, the boy said he had tried to get a date with Linda but failed. He also had written letters to her. Because of this he was a little bit worried. The police took away his clothes as well as those of Hay.

Two separate witnesses recalled hearing a scream from the cemetery about 10 p.m. A farmer's wife testified that she saw a couple standing in the cemetery, and had remarked to her husband that she had heard of courting couples in many places but not in a churchyard. A local farmer who had known Linda all her life stated that while passing Carwood Road in his van he had seen Linda. He had dogs in the back of his van and could not offer anyone in good clothes a lift; otherwise, he would have picked her up and taken her home.

Linda's father testified that on the day before her murder his daughter went to Huntfield to help with exercising ponies, returning home at about 4 p.m. The following day, Linda again went to Huntfield. He and his wife spent the day in Carluke. When they returned they found that their daughter was not at home. Worried, they contacted the police and a full-scale search began. Two constables found their daughter's body in the cemetery at 6.40 a.m.

She was lying partly under a yew tree beside a grave. A purse was near her head. There were bloodstains on the grass and blood on her head and cheek. A piece of string was found hanging from a nearby tree. Linda was lying on her back and her clothing was displaced. There was a deep weal round her neck which had broken the skin. Her anorak was bunched up under her head.

Detective-Sgt John Paton, who photographed the body, said there was bruising on the girl's breast which looked like bite marks. A doctor who examined the body said she was fully clothed but her upper garments had been drawn up, exposing the upper part of her body. Her lower garments were also drawn up. It appeared that a cord or string had been tightly tied round her neck.

Bank manager, Thomas Aitken, testified that while driving home he saw a young couple in his headlights near the cemetery. At home, he put on the television and heard Dickie Henderson introducing Frank Sinatra, Jun. on the *Blackpool Show*. He was later taken to Scottish Television's Glasgow studio where he saw a re-run of the programme, using a stop-watch to indicate the precise moment he first saw the programme. It showed that he first saw the programme about 10.20 p.m. It took 20 minutes to drive from the point where he had seen the young couple.

On the second day of the trial, a 15-year-old boy from Fife said he saw Hay in pyjamas, dressing gown and boots on the night of the murder. Later he saw the dressing gown and pyjamas lying on Hay's bed in the dormitory they shared. He fell asleep and was awakened by the door slamming. Hay was there with all his clothes on. His face was dirty and there was dirt on the knees of his jeans. His hair was dishevelled.

Another boy, who slept in the same dormitory, recalled finding a metal fishhook on the beach at Montrose. He brought it back to the school and put it on top of a wardrobe. He showed the hook to Hay, who said something about using it for fighting in Biggar.

He saw Hay that night taking part in a whist drive. Later, he watched *The Untouchables* on the television until about 9.55 p.m. He then went back to his dormitory but there was no one there. Because of something he had been told he looked for the hook but could not find it. The last time he saw it was the day before, when he had shown it to Hay.

He saw Hay's dressing gown and pyjamas on his bed. Feeling worried, and anxious to find the hook, he searched for Hay. He went through the dormitories, the games room, sitting room and dining room but Hay was not there.

Returning with another boy from his dormitory at about 10.15, he saw that Hay's dressing gown and pyjamas were still on his bed. Roughly ten minutes later, the two boys went to sleep.

The boy's most dramatic evidence described how he was woken up by the sound of the door slamming: 'I saw Gordon was there. He had his clothing on, light-coloured jeans and a school jersey. He had nothing on his feet but his socks. I don't think he knew I was awake.

His face was dirty. His hair was as if he had been out in the wind. It was blown all over the place. It was just like he had been out working in the garden and sweating and he drew his hand across his face. His knees were a bit dirty, just like he had been kneeling down.'

Hay put on his pyjamas and washed at the sink. He was acting quite normally. Just as he was getting into bed a member of the staff turned out the lights and said 'Goodnight'. Hay said 'Goodnight' back. Hay's room-mate awoke later when a car arrived bringing back their housemother. The three boys in the dormitory went to the window and spoke to her.

Hay's room-mate asked him where he had been; Hay denied he had been anywhere. The boy told Hay he had been looking for him; Hay asked him where he had looked and then said he had been in the bathroom. The next day, the boy found the metal hook in the bottom of the wardrobe and put it back on top.

When he was cross-examined, the boy admitted he had told lies to Hay's solicitor and to the police but said he was now telling the truth. Immediately after the murder he was not prepared to say anything that would implicate Hay but he later changed his mind.

A 23-year-old student, William Bennett, who was acting as temporary housemaster at the school that night, had been in charge of Hay's dormitory. He told the court how Hay had won a prize that night at a whist drive. Not later than 10.35 p.m Bennett went to the dormitory to turn out the lights. Hay had said 'Goodnight'. After 9.20 p.m. the staff were patrolling to see that the boys were getting ready for bed.

The deputy headmaster, Clifford Davies, who was in charge that night, said he saw Hay in his dressing gown about 9.45 p.m. There was usually a check on the boys at 10 p.m. but there was no check that night because of the whist drive.

Three days after the crime, Hay was transferred to Rossie Farm Approved School, Montrose where, four days later, the police arrived to interview him. The headmaster, Mr John Henderson, insisted on being present as the police questioned Hay from 10 p.m. until 3.30 a.m. He was prepared to intervene, he told the court, if Hay were treated unfairly.

Asked if he had occasion to intervene, Mr Henderson replied 'The boot was on the other foot. The boy was impertinent to the police. He was truculent and aggressive.'

The boy was later taken away to Lanark and was brought back to Rossie Farm, the following evening. Hay claimed his nose had been injured but Henderson saw no sign of an injury. It was not unusual for approved schoolboys to hint that they had been mishandled by the police. Henderson found nothing to merit investigation.

Dr James Imrie, a lecturer in forensic medicine at Glasgow University who examined Linda Peacock's body at the cemetery and also carried out the post-mortem, told the court there was a ligature mark round her neck as well as bruising and the mark of a ligature on the left wrist. There was an area of bruising over the left breast. He thought it was caused by a bite.

There were white spots in the centre of the bruising on the breast. Asked what form of tooth would cause such a mark, Dr Imrie replied, 'A tooth with a hollow in its cutting edge.'

In the doctor's opinion, Linda had died between 10 p.m. and midnight. She was a virgin. On her left wrist there was blackening due to scorching as well as a blister. There were also two lacerations and bruising on her head. The doctor had found bloodstains on a grey shirt and trousers belonging to Hay. He said he had seen many bites in connection with sexual assaults and had tested for saliva with varying results. No saliva test was taken in this case. Even if it had been taken it might not have helped. There was no sign of wetness on the skin.

He had not considered the possibility of identifying the assailant as a result of the bite. If he had seen obvious teeth marks he would have considered it possible to identify the assailant. At the time, he said, they did not have it in mind to use the bite as a means of identification. If he had thought of this, he would have sent for a dentist to look at the breast.

When he was shown a metal hook, he agreed it could have caused the girl's injuries, although there were many other blunt instruments which could have done so.

On the third day of the trial, Lord Grant was accompanied on the Bench by Lords Walker and Milligan. The proceedings were interrupted by a three-hour debate on the question of whether evidence arising from the warrant to take impressions of Hay's teeth for the third time was admissible or not. Retiring for only five minutes following the debate, the judges returned to announce that the evidence was indeed admissible.

A week after Hay's conviction, Lord Grant issued a written judgment on this important ruling, which depended upon the judges' finding that the warrant authorising the Crown to take impressions of Hay's teeth was valid. It had been argued that, since Hay was not present at the hearing of the petition for the warrant before the sheriff, it had been incompetently granted. Given that the Crown did not ask Hay's permission to take the third impression, the warrant would be illegal if it had not been competently granted. Had Hay been under arrest at the time, different considerations would have applied.

There was no doubt that a warrant to search premises was not illegal merely because the person concerned had not been apprehended or charged. The defence position, however, was that a search of premises was a very different matter from the possibly forcible invasion of the privacy of the person. Nor were there any reported cases of a warrant being granted to search the person.

Lord Grant said that although he was not persuaded that the difference was a matter of principle rather than degree a warrant to search the person should be granted only in very exceptional circumstances. Even if he was wrong in holding the warrant to be competent, he would have admitted the evidence, for in this case, by his committal to an approved school, Hay had largely ceased to be the master of his movements. In these very special circumstances, the Sheriff-Substitute was, in Lord Grant's opinion, justified in granting the warrant.

By the fourth day of the trial, the Crown had clearly shown that Hay was not around the school at the time of Linda Peacock's death. There was, however, little other evidence pointing to Hay as the assailant – until Professor Simpson electrified the court by confidently asserting that it was Hay's teeth which had caused the bite mark on the girl's breast.

Professor Simpson testified that he had 30 years' experience in forensic medicine and was consultant to New Scotland Yard. He had no dental qualifications but he had lectured all over the world on forensic odontology, had published articles on the subject, and was currently head of the Department of Forensic Medicine at London University: Impressive credentials to support the crucial evidence he was about to give.

The marks on the girl's breast, Professor Simpson stated, were undoubtedly human bite marks. There were four marks which he regarded as quite characteristic of the points of pressure of teeth.

A firm hold had been made and the teeth had made a very distinct impression. There was some degree of suction; the bite must have been a painful one. In more than 30 years' practice the professor had seen many bite marks, both in his own cases and in others shown to him. He had never seen a bite mark with better defined detail than this.

It was accepted and orthodox practice to make transparencies and superimpose them over photographs of the injuries printed to the same scale in order to see to what extent exact matching took place. The methods in the Hay case followed the usual pattern. Professor Simpson was shown photographs taken from plaster casts of Hay's teeth as well as transparencies superimposed on photographs of the bite marks. He told the court: 'I have looked at these with the greatest of care, as I commonly have to do with instruments of any kind in relation to marks on the skin.

I see on this couple of superimposed transparencies a number of points of comparison, two of which, in my experience, are quite remarkable and quite unique.

I would say that these two marks, in their position and in their character, and the other kind of mark which shows a scraping of the skin surface, for which I would require some explanation, are three quite exceptionally detailed marks.

The presence of these three in this position and with those details would carry me a long way towards feeling that this was an exact comparison. I would be satisfied that this set of teeth – whichever it was – was the set that caused those marks'.

He was satisfied that Hay's teeth caused the bite marks on the girl's breast. Under cross-examination the professor said a saliva test was another test that could be applied in such cases. Some people excreted blood in their saliva and it might be possible to group the blood.

Mr Stewart said it was agreed by experts that it was easier to prove that bite marks were *not* caused by a particular suspect than to prove that they *were*. Professor Simpson replied that less trouble was entailed in excluding certain teeth. Others had to be studied more closely.

The court was told that in fingerprints 16 points of comparison were required to conclusively identify a particular suspect. Asked if a similar claim could be made for forensic odontology, Professor Simpson replied that the number of points of comparison was not as great as in fingerprinting. There had been, for example, eight to ten points in an English case.

Detective-Inspector Osborne Butler, of the Identification Bureau of Glasgow City Police, told the court that he went through the 29 casts of impressions of teeth taken from pupils and staff at Loaningdale and found that only No 11, belonging to Hay, fitted the marks found on the girl's breast. When he superimposed transparencies of Hay's teeth on the bite mark he found 'a demonstrable matching.' Hollows on the upper and lower canines, he said, corresponded with the bite mark.

During cross-examination, Detective-Inspector Butler stated that the teeth marks were 'probably unique.' Asked if there would be any other teath in Great Britain which could have made the marks, he replied, 'I would be surprised to find that.' Mr Stewart asked, 'Are you going as far as to say this is conclusive?' Inspector Butler indicated no doubt when he replied, 'In my view, due to the characteristics in the teeth, this is conclusive.'

Evidence was then given by other dental experts, who described how plaster casts had been taken from teeth impressions at Glasgow Dental Hospital. Hay's dental record card was produced, showing he required four fillings. Large diagrams of his teeth were used in court to ensure the jury understood the technical aspects of the evidence.

Two policemen who timed a run from the yew tree in the cemetery back to the school said it took one minute 43 seconds.

Detective-Superintendent James Weir said that Hay's attitude was 'one of resentment' when he saw him at Rossie School. When he was asked to account for his movements, Hay said he had watched television, had a game of cards and then went up to the dormitory at about 10.15 p.m. Two boys were in the 'dorm' when he went in. Weir told Hay that his statement was in conflict with other statements. Later, when he asked Hay if he had left the school that night, the boy replied, 'No, I never left the school. I can't change my story now, sir.'

The most dramatic evidence in the case came to light on the fifth day of the trial when Dr John Warren Harvey, lecturer in dental surgery at Glasgow University, entered the witness box. He told the court how he had examined the canine teeth of no fewer than 342 junior soldiers two months after the murder. He was trying to ascertain whether any of their teeth compared with the bite marks on the dead girl.

He looked at more than 1,000 canine teeth in the mouths of the soldiers. Only two had pitted eye teeth and none had pits in opposite canine teeth. He spent more than 200 painstaking hours studying the 29 teeth impressions taken. Only the canine teeth of Hay corresponded with the peculiarly-shaped bite marks on the girl's breast.

Using himself as a guinea pig, Dr Harvey demonstrated to the jury various bite marks. By pressing a copper impression of Hay's canine teeth against his finger he produced the peculiar pale-centred mark which was found on the girl's body. Using a small stick he produced from his pocket, he showed the jury the mark left by a solid object. Then, using a ball-point pen, he showed the court the mark left by a hollow-ended object.

Using Hay's upper right canine tooth, he showed that it left a mark on his finger which was pale in the centre and reddened round about.

When asked by the Solicitor-General if he could go any further than saying it was *possible* that Hay's mouth caused the bite marks, Dr Harvey said, 'I find it extremely difficult to conceive that another mouth would have this number of extraordinary characteristics.'

He said there was a broken edge on one tooth and a hook effect where part of a filling was missing. These were remarkable characteristics when taken together. The mark just below the nipple was quite unlike any mark he had ever seen described in forensic literature.

Dr Harvey described how he had been contacted by Inspector Butler while on holiday in Ireland. Returning to Scotland, he was given 29 plaster models of teeth from impressions. They were identified by number only.

He was able to eliminate 24, leaving five, including, as it was later revealed, the impression of Hay's teeth. A second set of impressions was taken. From these, Dr Harvey was able to exclude another four-leaving only No 11. The small pits he found in the tips of the upper and lower canines were 'quite dramatic and extraordinary.' He had never seen marks made by teeth which left a pale centre. It was something quite unusual.

Re-examining all 29 of the impressions taken, Dr Harvey found one set which answered the problem of the gaps and the abrasions or tears in the skin. The set which made these extraordinary marks was No 11.

It was at this stage that he decided to make perfectly certain by using different materials and techniques to obtain a third, more finely-detailed impression. A warrant to take the final impression of Hay's teeth was subsequently granted.

Under cross-examination, Dr Harvey told the court that 80 per cent of the people in court might have hollows in their teeth but these were completely different from the strange pits in Hay's teeth. Asked if he could exclude the possibility of another mouth in Great Britain making the bite marks, he said he would find it extremely difficult to believe that such a mouth existed.

After more than five hours in the witness box, the doctor was unshaken in his conviction that the bite marks on Linda Peacock's body were made by Hay.

On the sixth day of the trial, Gordon Hay spent more than two hours in the witness box. Looking perfectly cool, çalm and collected, he strongly denied that he was out of the school on the night Linda Peacock was murdered. He did agree, however, that he had left the school a few times to meet girls when he was not supposed to be out. He also agreed that he told lies in several of the statements he made to the police. He denied that his two room-mates were his alibi. The two boys he claimed, were telling lies and Mr Davies, the deputy headmaster, must be mistaken if he said he last saw him at 9.45 p.m. that night. Hay told the court he had been convicted of breaking and entering at Aberdeen Sheriff Court in December 1966 and arrived at Loaningdale Approved School in January 1967. He said he had never been convicted of assault.

He had seen Linda Peacock in Biggar a couple of times but had never spoken to her. The day before she was murdered, he went with two other boys and a master to the pictures in

Biggar; that evening, they went to a fair. A girl came across and spoke to one of the boys. He did not know her at the time but he now knew it was Linda Peacock. He did not speak to her at all. Asked if he had said he would not mind going out with Linda, Hay replied, 'Yes.'

Hay said that he remembered another boy producing a metal hook and saying he was going to get someone with it. He told the boy he would only get into trouble and took the hook from him and threw it on top of a cupboard. The next time he saw the hook was in court.

He also denied saying to anyone that he intended going to Biggar, and claimed never to have left the school at all that evening. He had won a prize at a whist drive in the school and, before supper, changed into a white shirt with his pyjama bottoms. He did not think he had a dressing gown on. He was wearing his boots as he did not like the school sandals. After supper, he watched *The Untouchables* on television, which finished at 9.55 p.m. He then went to the dining room to watch a game of cards. At 10.02 p.m. he spoke to another boy and they checked their watches. He spoke to another boy for ten or fifteen minutes, returning to his dormitory between 10.15 and 10.30 p.m. One of his room-mates was already there; the second came in afterwards.

They got into bed and a member of the staff turned out the lights. Later the boys spoke to the housemother when she arrived back by car and then listened to the radio, which was switched off about midnight. Hay denied having had a conversation the next day with one of the boys about what they would tell the police concerning the murder.

Hay recalled being visited by detectives at Rossie School after he had been transferred there. They greeted him: 'Hello, Gordon. You weren't expecting to see us again, were you?'

They said to him in the presence of the headmaster: 'We know you did it, Gordon. Why not admit it?'

When the detectives went out, Hay was left alone with the headmaster, who told him: 'They know you did it. I know you did it. Why not admit it?'

After being taken to Lanark, he was returned to Rossie, where he told the headmaster, 'My nose was skinned.' The headmaster asked him what had happened and he told him a detective had hit him. He also told the headmaster the police banged his head against a wall a couple of times and put him in a cell. They kept trying to get him to admit it.

Mr Ewan Stewart, cross-examing, said, 'You are just lying to try to blacken everyone?' But Hay denied this.

Hay agreed he had sneaked out of the school and back again without the staff finding out. But he denied he had his eye on Linda. He admitted he had not always told the same story about his movements that night.

During the rigorous cross-examination, Hay remained completely unruffled, putting on an altogether calm and convincing performance. Re-examined by his own counsel, he again denied he was out of the school that night and denied killing Linda.

On the final day of the hearing of evidence, a dental expert called for the defence threw a small spanner in the works when he cast doubt on the significance of the bite marks. Professor George Beagrie, Professor of Restorative Dentistry at Edinburgh University, said he found it difficult to determine what the Crown experts meant by their statements that defects in canine teeth were rare.

He had carried out an experiment with 50 teeth impressions from his own department and found teeth with pits similar to those which the Crown said Hay's teeth showed. He accepted that the bite mark could have been made by Hay but he did not feel it was beyond reasonable doubt. The incidence of defective canine teeth was greater than the Crown experts said. He felt that there could be other mouths in Great Britain that could have caused the bite marks.

Addressing the jury, the Solicitor-General said the case had 'some unusual features'. A certain amount of evidence against Hay was dental and pathological evidence concerning the bite marks. It was clear from the dental evidence, he said, that the only set of teeth out of the 29 that could have made the bite was Hay's.

He said there was no criticism of Linda Peacock of a sexual character. She was not sexually promiscuous. The jury might think it was highly unlikely that she would go voluntarily into the graveyard with some stray tramp who just chanced to meet her on the road. She would only have accompanied someone she knew to that place.

Hay, he said, must have 'worn the cloak of invisibility' for he had not been seen after 9.50 p.m. by six of the masters at his school. His alibi should thus be rejected, root and branch.

When he came to deal with forensic odontology, Mr Stewart said: 'We are not dabbling in some kind of experimental matter. There have been cases on the Continent and in England in which this form of identification has been used. But even supposing there were other people with this kind of mouth existing in the world or even in Britain, how many of these people had on August 5 been expressing a sexual interest in Linda Peacock? How many were living within two minutes of the cemetery? How many were sneaking back into their beds about ten minutes after the murder with their hair blown about and dirt on their faces and clothing? How many had in their possession an instrument such as a hook? How many of these people were next day trying to get their friends to tell lies? There is only one verdict here which an objective and just appraisal and evaluation of the evidence can lead to — a verdict of guilty.'

Mr Ian Stewart, for the defence, said this was the first case of its kind in Scotland in which forensic odontology had been used. In Britain this science was in its infancy. Sixteen characteristics were required in fingerprints but that was not the case here. In Britain, he said, the experience of the dental profession was very limited in this type of case. Only one dentist had said it was beyond reasonable doubt that Hay's teeth caused the bite marks.

The fact that Hay had lied on occasion and may have lied in evidence did not make him the murderer, Mr Stewart argued. If the Crown broke Hay's alibi that still did not make him the murderer. The evidence for the Crown was circumstantial; the case was balanced 'on a knife edge.' The only evidence that connected Hay with the crime and, moreover, with the scene of the crime, was related to bite marks.

In his two-hour charge to the jury, gravel-voiced Lord Grant warned that circumstantial evidence was not enough to convict Hay. 'For that reason,' he said, 'the dental and pathological evidence is of paramount importance. This forensic odontology, as it is called, is a relatively new science but there must, of course, always be a first time.'

Lord Grant reminded the jury that scientific and medical knowledge advanced as the years went on. It was only comparatively recently that fingerprints had come to be accepted as infallible. It was only in 1945 that palm prints had been recognised. It was of importance that the law should keep pace with science.

Lord Grant said that the case was, as well as a grave one, in some ways unique, difficult and puzzling. But he thought it right to say that he and the jury had been assisted in their task by the way in which it had been prepared and also by the admirable presentation by the Solicitor-General, Mr Ewan Stewart and his colleague, Mr Ian Stewart, for the defence.

Lord Grant pointed out to the jury that even if Hay had told lies that was not sufficient to establish his guilt. They must therefore examine the evidence on the bite marks with care and in the light of their assessment of the expert witnesses. In assessing the evidence, he continued, the jury should keep in mind that the Crown experts had both made a special study of forensic odontology. The two experts for the defence, on the other hand, were being pushed rather beyond the field where their own expert knowledge lay.

The judge's dismissal of the defence experts' evidence was probably a crucial factor in the jury's deliberations and must have removed any doubts in their minds about the strength and weight of the scientific evidence for the Crown.

After an absence of two and a half hours, the jury returned a majority verdict of 'Guilty'. The judge ordered Hay to be detained during Her Majesty's pleasure as he was under 18 when he committed the crime.

Hay showed no emotion as he was led away. Sitting in court were his grey-haired mother, Mrs Hannah Hay, and the mother of his victim, Mrs Mary Peacock.

Mrs Hay said afterwards that her husband, Robert, a farm labourer, died on the day after Gordon's 16th birthday. 'Up till then, Gordon was fairly happy and content but I think his dad's death had an effect on him. After that, I saw an awful change in my boy. He seemed to go completely off the rails.'

Gordon wrote to his mother twice a week while he was awaiting trial. His mother said: 'I always looked forward to his letters. He's my son and I can forgive him although I can never believe he did this terrible thing. I will stand by him.'

Gordon Hay was a country-born boy who loved cars and often boasted about girl friends. His love of cars got him into trouble and led to him being sent to an approved school. He danced well and was admired by the girls but friends said he was basically a loner.

Linda's parents, however, could never forget or forgive. Her father said afterwards the school should never have been in Biggar at all and that he would support any move to have it closed down.

Mrs Peacock spoke of her ordeal and her bitterness. 'Linda was a lovely young girl whose life was cut short viciously by a boy from that school,' she said.

It was the third time that tragedy had struck the Peacock family. Two years earlier, Linda's elder sister died after an illness and a year before that her uncle, a ship's cook, drowned in a dockside accident in England.

Hay's appeal two months later in the Court of Criminal Appeal in Edinburgh was heard by a bench of five judges because of the important legal question of whether the sheriff had the right to issue the warrant to take further teeth impressions from Hay before he was charged.

Lord Clyde, Lord Justice General, presided with Lords Guthrie, Migdale, Cameron and Johnston.

Mr Ian Stewart, in a strong argument, contended that the dental evidence obtained under the warrant was inadmissable and was prejudicial to Hay. The police were not entitled to search the person of a suspect before arrest, he claimed. His argument was particularly concerned with the search of a person as a means of identification rather than to find objects in his possession.

Police powers on identification were limited to such observation as was possible without interfering with the person. Interference with the person without consent and before the individual's arrest was technically as assault. It was a principle of Scottish criminal law that you could not search a person before arresting him.

Mr Stewart argued that there is always a conflict between the rights of an individual and the rights of the state. The right of the state to override the rights of the individual was a matter on which Parliament alone should legislate; it was not for the court to overrule a principle of personal liberty established for many years.

The Solicitor-General argued for the Crown that although the warrant in question was unique there was nothing unlawful about it. If the court could not accept that proposition, the circumstances in the case were such that an irregularity fell to be excused.

Moreover, there was a general power for magistrates to grant warrants for the advancement of the course of justice. In the present case, there had been insufficient evidence to put Hay on trial and the Crown wished to confirm further evidence. The warrant, the Solicitor-General argued, was perfectly valid in the special circumstances. There was no unfairness. Everything was done in the public interest and in the interests of the accused.

The five judges rejected the appeal and on 30 May 1968 gave their reasons. Lord Clyde said that although Hay was not present or legally represented at the hearing for the warrant, the presence of an independent judicial officer, such as the sheriff, afforded the basis for a fair reconciliation of the interests of the public in the suppression of crime and of the individual, who was entitled not to have the liberty of his person or premises unduly jeopardised.

The hearing before the sheriff was by no means a formality; the court had to be satisfied that the circumstances justified the unusual course that had been taken and that the warrant was not too wide or oppressive. The sheriff was the safeguard against the granting of too general a warrant. A warrant of this limited kind would, however, be granted only in special circumstances.

The judge held that the warrant was quite legal and the resulting evidence therefore admissible. Apart from anything else, there was in this case an element of urgency; a visit to the dentist or an injury to Hay's teeth could have destroyed the evidence.

After the conviction, there was a public outcry against the approved school. Biggar Town Council demanded it should be closed immediately or, at least, that the whole staff from the headmaster down should be changed. Provost James Telfer said that since 1963, when Loaningdale opened, the town had wanted a public inquiry into the running of the school. 'We got it during the trial. The security there was terrible,' he said.

In 1965, the Town Council, worried by a spate of petty crimes, demanded a meeting with the school's board of managers. It was an experimental school set up to rehabilitate young boys. A spokesman for the Scottish Education Department said at the time that it was not a penal institution to keep children permanently out of the community. Only boys who were thought capable of returning to society in a matter of months were to be admitted to the school.

Security at Loaningdale was tightened in January 1968, after the council met Mr Bruce Millan, the Under-Secretary of State responsible for education. A night alarm system was installed to alert staff to any break-out. If any boy left the school without permission he was immediately sent to a stricter establishment. But Councillor James Stephen summed up the feelings of local people when he said, 'There is no doubt that this experiment has failed. You cannot cure a bad boy by permissiveness. And when prizes of cigarettes are given out at whist drives and 13-year-olds are allowed to smoke, the whole thing is ridiculous.'

The headmaster, who was on holiday at the time of the murder, was in favour of trying to rehabilitate young offenders. He allowed smoking in the school and allowed the boys to call masters by their Christian names. He recommended Hay's transfer to another school because he did not think he was suitable for Loaningdale.

Provost Telfer, who joined the board of the school in 1965 after the first row, said, 'If it was left to the people of Biggar, it would be closed immediately. There is a tremendous amount of ill-feeling in the town about it. Since the murder, there has been a fantastic amount of complaints by people who have not voiced them before.'

Councillor Stephen, who canvassed more than 20,000 signatures for his petition calling for the return of the death penalty, said the Loaningdale experiment — it was the first 'open' type of school in Scotland — had failed lamentably. The petty dictators of St Andrews House, he said, had decreed it would be sited at Biggar regardless of local feeling.

A spokesman for the Social Work Services Group at the

Scottish Office said: 'There have been, and always will be, enormous difficulties in rehabilitating young people who have been out of step with society. It is difficult to talk about success or failure in a social education context.'

At the time, there were 36 boys in Loaningdale: 31 for theft, three for truancy and two for road traffic offences. This did not suggest the school was harbouring would-be killers.

After the meeting with Mr Millan, two more local people, a doctor and a minister, were added to the board of the school, of which Lord Birsay was chairman.

A Government spokesman summed up the difficulties of rehabilitation when he said: 'Selection is a basic part of the experiment. A boy's record, IQ, family history and condition are all considered. In addition, great weight is given to an assessment of the willingness of a family to co-operate in treatment and of inter-family relationships.'

Linda Peacock's parents at first considered suing the Scottish Education Department, who were responsible for selection of the boys sent to the school. Eventually, however, they accepted £2,000 compensation from the Criminal Injuries Board.

Mrs Peacock said:

> The money is no compensation for Linda's life. We are more interested in punishment for all those responsible for the negligent system that led to her death. We had considered a civil action but have now dropped that as the only measure a civil court might take would be to award damages, which is little comfort to us.

Writing in the Glasgow Police magazine some time later, Dr Warren Harvey, in an article called 'The Tooth, the Whole Truth and the Police' revealed that 25 dentists were now linked with the police in Aberdeen, Dundee, Edinburgh and Glasgow to help in criminal cases. When a victim is bitten, Harvey wrote, the marks must be seen at the first possible moment by a dentist, a police photographer and a pathologist. He pointed out that the Biggar murder trial verdict was by a majority of 14 to 1 and that about one third of the 1,100 foolscap pages in the transcript of the evidence consisted of dental and medical evidence.

But, a few years later, allegations by an internationally

known expert on forensic odontology, Dr Soren Keiser-Nielsen of the Department of Forensic Odontology at the Royal Dental College in Copenhagen, cast a slight shadow over the new science. He alleged that he came to Scotland before the trial but his evidence had been 'hushed up' and he had been hurriedly got out of the way. In a letter to the Forensic Society's journal, he said he concluded there was nothing in the mark on the victim's breast to indicate it was a bite mark. Even if it were, he added, there were too few points of similarity to warrant a dental identification of the originator. He had explained his reasoning and conclusions, and asked whether the fact he had drawn conclusions adverse to the Crown case would come to the notice of the defence.

But the Crown revealed that the doctor had considered the evidence insufficient to justify a firm conclusion on identification and had declined to give evidence. Counsel for the defence had accordingly been informed by the Crown that Dr Keiser-Neilsen was not willing to give evidence.

The Crown also said the doctor's views expressed at the time did not match the views he expressed later. He had undoubtedly withdrawn, declining to give evidence. Mr Alistair R. Brownlie, Secretary of the Society of Solicitors in the Supreme Courts of Scotland, strongly denied the doctor's allegations. The doctor, Mr Brownlie maintained, had indicated he wanted nothing more to do with the case and was therefore not called as a witness. The police who drove him to the airport were merely exercising the customary courtesies. The doctor was not, as he later claimed, hurriedly got out of the way.

But the controversy still did not die down. Keiser-Nielsen insisted in 1972 that the mark on Linda Peacock's breast was not a human bite mark. Hay's counsel, Mr Ian Stewart, recalled being told the doctor was not prepared to come and give evidence and that there was no point in calling him as a witness if he was unwilling to come.

While there is little likelihood of compulsory dental examination becoming a standard feature of Scottish pre-trial criminal procedure, the courts clearly recognised the exceptional nature of the case in approving the warrant to take the vital third impression of Hay's teeth. The power given to the prosecution to secure that important evidence from the previously inviolable person of the suspect might well be used again if the course of justice demands it.

Had genetic fingerprinting, which has been hailed as the greatest breakthrough in forensic science this century, been available at that time, even more conclusive proof might well have been provided by the scientists.

CHAPTER 3
Operation Mullet

A 5p phone call from a businessman in Edinburgh brought about the downfall of a multi-million pound Dutch drugs syndicate who were running an illicit drugs laboratory at a remote country cottage in Scotland. They were producing methyl amphetamine, popularly known as speed, but it was believed they were on the verge of unlocking the secret of manufacturing synthetic cocaine.

Mr Alan Hepburn, the 39-year-old managing director of a city firm, informed the police when his company received an order for 10 kilograms of BMK–benzyl methyl ketone. The chemical was a special compound, any sales of which were to be notified to the Home Office. Hepburn was told to go ahead with the delivery and the chemical, which could be used to make amphetamines, was collected by a member of the drugs ring at a cost of £655.

Lothian and Borders Police, Tayside Police, Interpol, the Dutch police and the Central Drugs Intelligence Unit at New Scotland Yard, who co-ordinate all information about drugs activity in the UK, all co-operated in uncovering the biggest illicit drugs operation ever to come to light in Scotland.

The investigation over many months led to round-the-clock surveillance by the police. In a dawn raid on 30 September, 1979, at remote, white-washed Cleves Cottage, two miles from West Linton, Peeblesshire, they found what was described as 'a chemical Aladdin's Cave' with a potential to produce more than £70 million worth of amphetamines.

The investigation, codenamed 'Operation Mullet' after, while in a fishing trip, the head of the police drugs squad caught a red mullet and thought it was strange and slippery like the foreign nationals he was investigating. It followed 'Operation Julie' in England, where millions of pounds worth of drug-making chemicals had been seized.

The Dutch syndicate's operation in Scotland was complex and well-organised. A legitimate company, Greenways Products, was set up from a bungalow in Affleck Gardens, Monikie, near Dundee. Membership of Dundee Chamber of Commerce was even used as a front to allay any suspicion, and their telex link was used to order chemicals from companies all over Britain and the Continent.

The scientific brains behind it all was a brilliant 28-year-old chemist, Jan Stuurman, whose aims in life had become misguided. Clever and plausible, he never completed his chemistry degree in Holland as his final studies were interrupted by a prison sentence.

Stuurman was jailed for a year in 1971 and for two years in 1973. In 1976 he teamed up with Dick Ruiter, whom he had met in prison, to produce amphetamines at Andijk in Holland. Stuurman contributed his scientific and computer knowledge and Ruiter the expertise of a trained maintenance engineer. Ruiter became Stuurman's faithful mechanic, handyman, gardener and chauffeur.

A small-time operator in Amsterdam gave them their chance to become the drug kings of Europe by arming them with false passports. They fled from Holland, where they were wanted by the police, with Stuurman's wife, Reinette, on a tour of the drugs capitals of the world, visiting Sri Lanka, Indonesia, Colombia and Switzerland before arriving in Scotland to set up their drugs factory.

International financial backers gave them £50,000 to set up their laboratory but grew impatient as time passed with no return on their money by way of the production of synthetic cocaine. Only then did the ring decide to produce amphetamines as a 'cash crop' while the slower process of manufacturing cocaine could be started. In the rais on Cleves Cottage, nearly 3,000 grammes of methyl amphetamine, mixed with other chemicals, was found. Swift police action forestalled the final process of turning the liquid into tablet or pill form, which would have been worth about £3 million on the black market.

The modern bungalow in Monikie had become the suburban front for Stuurman and Ruiter's European drugs organisation. During many months of police surveillance, both at the cottage and at the bungalow, the merest hint that the police were on to them would have blown the whole case. Only those police officers who needed to know were allowed into the secret of the long surveillance. The secrecy even extended to the uniformed officers involved.

When Stuurman rented Cleves Cottage, he explained to the local farmer who owned it that he would be working late at night and needed peace and quiet. He paid £65 a month rent. Silent and secretive at the cottage, the Dutchmen were open and friendly at Monikie. Hiding behind foreign aliases, Stuurman, his wife and Ruiter settled down to enjoy middle-class respectability in their bungalow, using it as their business address when they set up their company in October 1978, shortly after they arrived in Scotland.

At the bungalow, both Stuurman and Ruiter worked hard at presenting an image of successful and suave business partners in an expanding firm engaged in chemical research. So self-confident was Stuurman that he held a 'getting-to-know-you' party for the neighbours. He mixed regularly with local businessmen and even managed to be elected a member of Dundee Chamber of Commerce.

Stuurman was on the verge of a breakthrough that would have sent the drugs world into orbit: man-made cocaine. Using two computers, he had already worked out a formula for the drug by the time of the police raid. Fortunately, he did not have enough time to experiment with production, and no one has yet found the secret of synthetic cocaine.

When they were experimenting in Holland in 1977, Stuurman and Ruiter were foolish enough to take a sample of their end-product to a public analyst, who tipped off the authorities that they had been producing methyl amphetamine.

A police forensic expert described the scene in their laboratory in an outhouse at the cottage as 'fantastic'. A senior police officer said there was enough chemical material there to produce £100 million worth of illicit drugs. The implications, he said, were frightening. If they had gone into full-scale production drugs would have flooded Europe. The police were convinced that a computer print-out found on a window-sill which contained a formula for synethic cocaine described the next stage in production.

When the police raided the cottage at dawn they found a virtual fortress. There was an elaborate alarm system fixed to the garden gate and a false wall leading to a sealed part of the loft. There was a strong smell of chemicals. A freshly-dug hole, 12' by 8', was found in the garden. Wires led from the garden gate to the garage, the kitchen and to the small adjoining building where they found the laboratory. When the gate was opened, a buzzer sounded in the kitchen and a bell in the laboratory. Switches in the kitchen and the laboratory enabled the system to be used to signal from one to the other.

The cottage had a fine vantage point overlooking the south for quite a distance and the police had great difficulty keeping the gang under surveillance using high-powered binoculars. In the garage they found a ladder and at the top of the wall there was a 2½' square gap in the brickwork leading into the loft, where there were containers and cardboard boxes full of chemicals. An ingenious piece of brickwork fitted on rollers could be pulled into the hole to seal off the loft.

Stuurman, Ruiter and a third man, 34-year-old Albertus Merks, were arrested at the scene and Mrs Stuurman was arrested at the bungalow. Merks was described as the European supervisor and courier of the operation. All four were charged with producing methyl amphetamine or with being lawfully concerned in the production of the drug. Another charge alleged they were in possession of 2,925 grammes of the drug, with intent to supply it to another. Mrs Stuurman was also charged with unlawfully having cannabis and cannabis resin in her possession.

Their arrest led to the *Glasgow Herald* being fined £20,000 and its editor £750 for contempt of court. Radio Forth was also fined £10,000 and its chief executive £1,000.

Lord Justice General Emslie was scathing in his condemnation of the newspaper, whose report on the drugs ring gave a wealth of detail on the police investigation and alleged evidence of a highly incriminating nature, tending to suggest the guilt of those arrested might be presumed. The newspaper even revealed that three of those arrested had escaped from a Dutch jail although, in fact, only Stuurman and Ruiter had escaped.

Lord Emslie said the contempt was of the gravest character and was well-nigh incomprehensible. Even an inexperienced journalist would have known it would constitute contempt of the gravest kind. The judges were appalled to learn the newspaper had taken legal advice. The Herald later brought an action for £24,000 damages against their legal advisers over the information they were given in the drugs case. The case was later settled.

Alleging there had been prejuddicial publicity at the time of their arrest, all four accused made a plea that their trial should not go ahead. But three judges in the High Court in Edinburgh rejected their plea and decided the trial should begin.

Lord Avonside, who presided, said nothing had been said to persuade them that the contempt by the newspaper and in a Radio Forth broadcast was of such a nature as to amount to oppression by the Lord Advocate in proceeding with the trial. They did not consider the accused would be denied a fair trial under proper directions by the trial judge.

When the trial began in the High Court in Edinburgh on 28 January 1980, Stuurman denied they were producing illicit drugs at their laboratory and claimed he was harmlessly engaged in a search for a synthetic version of indigo blue, the dye used in jeans. Unknown to the jury, this was the same plea he had made in Holland when he was accused of a similar operation there in 1977.

A British Oxygen representative, John McDonald, told the court that a Mr Larson, whom he identified as Stuurman, placed an order for hydrogen chloride which was a 'hazardous gas.' Mr McDonald explained that he wanted to make sure the gas would be used in the correct manner and under correct supervision and was not too happy that the order came from a private house at Dundee. But Stuurman told him he had a laboratory in the Borders and was going to use it there. Stuurman said he was the brains behind the operation. After placing the order Stuurman asked for another special gas which was also hazardous. Stuurman explained to McDonald that his firm made small quantities of chemicals as one-off orders and also sold computer software.

Mr McDonald said he saw a room at the bungalow packed with electrical equipment, including visual display units. After his report his company was satisfied and the orders went through. Stuurman told him he had designed the software for computerising chemicals.

The 29-year-old area sales manager of Re-Chem International Ltd of Larbert, Cornelius Ferguson, said he was asked by Greenway Products to give a quotation for the disposal of four 44-gallon drums of toxic chemical waste each month. The waste contained three different kinds of toxic chemicals. He quoted them £105 a ton and a pick-up fee of £40 but never heard from the company again.

The court was told that a Barry Groenewegen, an alias said to have been used by Stuurman, produced a Dutch passport when he opened an account in the Royal Bank, High Street, Dundee in May 1979. He deposited £4,000 and over the next four months changed £16,000 worth of Dutch florins, Swiss and French francs and US dollars for sterling.

Police forensic scientist John Gillespie said the material found at the cottage could be diluted to produce up to £60 million worth of tablets of amphetamine but many of the drugs found at the laboratory strongly indicated the attempted production of synthetic cocaine. He could not believe his eyes when he saw the equipment in the laboratory. He respected Stuurman for his (albeit misdirected) scientific knowledge and discounted the theory that the laboratory was being used for research into a synthetic indigo dye.

Mr Gillespie spent a fortnight at the cottage testing materials found there. Inside the laboratory, he found a wide range of scientific equipment, all linked by tubing. Water and electricity had been connected from the cottage and there were cylinders of nitrogen and hydrogen gases. The production of the amphetamines had been a full-scale operation, studied in great depth and meticulously planned. However, a vast quantity of the chemicals and equipment found had nothing whatsoever to do with the manufacture of amphetamines. There was evidence of in-depth research into cocaine. The gang had designed a very elaborate system which was not really required for methyl amphetamine.

A computer expert told the court that 'a vast amount' of coded information relating to chemicals was found with two computers at the cottage.

Mrs Martha Haining, the Stuurmans' next-door neighbour at Monikie, said she knew them as Barry and Nettie Groenewegen. Ruiter, who also lived there, she knew as 'Ton'.

She saw packages and parcels being delivered and was told they were something to do with computers. She saw a man they called 'The Boss' arrive at the house on two occasions. She identified him as Merks.

Ruiter testified that he had lived in Holland until 1977, working as a mechanic and as the proprietor of an inn. He had run into tax problems, like Stuurman, and had to sell the inn. He bought a false passport in Amsterdam because the police had confiscated his own. He then went on a world tour with the Stuurmans. He arrived in Scotland in September 1978 and stayed with the Stuurmans. He returned to Switzerland but later received a letter from Stuurman inviting him to join his business. He returned to Scotland and worked as a mechanic to maintain the laboratory equipment. He understood Stuurman was trying to make indigo blue and it never occurred to him that he was manufacturing amphetamines or drugs of any kind.

The removable section of brickwork which sealed off part of the loft at the cottage was a safety measure. Chemicals were stored there and the garage door was easily opened. An alarm system was installed so they would know if there was a danger of their dog running out on to the road. It was 'a very great surprise', Ruiter claimed, when the police raided the cottage and he was arrested.

Merks told the court he ran two businesses from his home in Holland. He had an antiques business and was also a commission agent, buying and selling things. In 1978 Stuurman asked him to collect a piece of equipment in Germany and to deliver it to him at Cambridge. Stuurman and Ruiter met him there. He first visited Dundee on a social visit in September 1979 but later made a second trip to deliver a piece of equipment from a German firm. He waited for his commission to arrive and was 'bored stiff'. Stuurman asked him not to go into the laboratory, as he was a smoker and might light a cigarette without thinking.

Stuurman, bearded and wearing spectacles, entered the witness box on the tenth day of the trial. He spoke softly in excellent English. He said he studied chemistry for four years at university in Amsterdam and this led to a job in which he specialised in producing computer programmes for nuclear power plants. He resigned in 1978 to go into private research combining his chemistry and computer expertise and formed several companies.

By the end of 1977, by which time he had made some profit, he got two calls from income tax inspectors. He had two options: either to sell everything he had and pay the taxes or to sell everything, take the money, and go abroad. With about £60,000 he tried unsuccessfully to set up business in underdeveloped countries in the Far East before trying his luck in Scotland.

He entered Britain using the name Groenewegen and then changed it to Larson when he heard the tax authorities had discovered his alias. He maintained that his work in Scotland was to seek a synthesis for an indigo blue dye.

Mr Ranald McLean (now Lord MacLean), QC for the Crown, had conducted a meticulous case for the prosecution. He told the jury it was odd that both Stuurman and Ruiter had given the same excuse for obtaining false passports and leaving Holland — that they were both fleeing from the taxman. The cost of the operation at Cleves Cottage was £40,000 and in one year Stuurman had had no return. Mr MacLean remarked:

> I suppose scientific research is an uphill struggle and the big breakthrough in the indigo blue discovery may have been just around the corner. This is the substance we have heard in evidence that costs £2,000 a ton — compared with legally manufactured methyl amphetamine, which costs £100 a gramme. What is the explanation? I suggest there is none.

Referring to the Aladdin's Cave of chemicals in the loft, he said no doubt the genie from the lamp was called drugs:

> At the end of the day, a picture emerges which you could call the Dutch Connection. Stuurman and Ruiter knew each other well. They travelled abroad together and not by accident. Stuurman at least knew Merks and I suggest to you that they met in Colombia in 1978. The decision was a joint one between the four of them to base their operations in Scotland because of the wide open spaces and easy access to Holland.
>
> They were funded from abroad and the immediate project was to produce methyl amphetamine, probably for European

distribution. Merks, I suggest, was the European supervisor of the operation. It was after Merks arrived from Europe that there was an increase in the activity at Cleves Cottage and it was obvious that this was because of the very great desire to get the product out.

The police forensic scientists have described as nonsense Stuurman's claim that they were searching for a synthetic dye. There was no evidence of any research on paper or in articles about indigo blue but there were articles on methyl amphetamine. There was also detailed research into cocaine and LSD.

Mr MacLean dropped the cannabis charge against Mrs Stuurman but she still remained accused of being unlawfully concerned in the production of methyl amphetamine.

Mr Lionel Daiches, Q.C. for Stuurman, said the case had been a difficult, arduous and important one. He hoped to show that none of the charges against Stuurman had been established in any real way at all. He said:

> The whole Crown case proceeds on the supposition that right from the start it had been a conspiracy by European rogues to form a big manufacturing cartel in a remote part of Scotland to make enormous profits to send back to Europe. But the Crown have completely failed to establish this element of furtiveness, illegality and this element of clandestine operation.

Prosecution witnesses, Mr Daiches argued, had selected only the sinister purposes of the chemicals found and had forgotten all about their multifarious innocent purposes.

Mr Raymond Fraser, for Ruiter, said Stuurman was the only chemist and it was only his brain that contained the key to the 'bubble bubble' and only one mind could produce the drug. 'Stuurman,' Mr Fraser said, was the Dutch word for 'helmsman' or 'one who steered'. The evidence had clearly shown it was Stuurman who had guided and steered the operation throughout:

> He was the only Dr Frankenstein in this particular laboratory because his was the only mind sufficiently gifted to be able to being into existence the monster he created and, like such a character, he had to have the assistance of a capable laboratory technician. In Ruiter, he found a man of considerable excellence but there is nothing to suggest they were 'equal partners in this enterprise'.

The Crown case against Ruiter, Mr Fraser argued, was based purely on speculation and suspicion. He was a mechanical engineering wizard being highly paid for his skilled work.

Mr Ranald Sutherland, QC, (now a High Court judge), for Merks, said his client was a legitimate businessman travelling on his own passport. He was not involved in setting up the laboratory. He was waiting for his money at Cleves Cottage after delivering equipment and was not performing any useful purpose in the laboratory. The Crown description of him as the European supervisor and courier was rather fanciful.

After the three-week trial, the jury took just over an hour to return unanimous verdicts against all three men. On the judge's direction, Mrs Stuurman was acquitted on all charges. The judge ruled there was insufficient evidence to convict her of being unlawfully concerned in the production of the drug.

She said afterwards: 'I am very pleased to be free. It has been a very anxious time.'

Stuurman and Ruiter were both convicted of producing methyl amphetamine between September 1978 and September 1979. Merks was convicted of being unlawfully concerned in the production of the drug. All three were also convicted of posessing 2,849 grammes of the drug, with intent to supply another.

Lord Allanbridge passed sentences totalling 75 years on the three men. He passed sentences of 12 years, 10 years and 3 years on each of the three charges against them, to run concurrently. It was expected they would each serve most of their 12-year sentences in prison in Scotland before being returned to the Dutch authorities.

The judge said the case was probably the most serious ever dealt with in Scotland under the Misuse of Drugs Act. He gave each of the convicted men equal sentences as he was satisfied that all three were engaged in their separate ways in criminal activities which could not be tolerated in Scotland and which it was incumbent upon the courts to do all they could to eradicate.

He entirely agreed with the police forensic report that the complete operation had been carefully researched and meticulously planned. He commended all the police involved.

From the time suspicions were first aroused, he said, the handling of the investigation by every single officer concerned merited the highest praise. Any false move would have alerted the criminals but, in the event, the net of 'Operation Mullet' had closed in upon the criminals.

The gang produced £3 million worth of amphetamines in an impure, liquid form but the vast amount of chemicals found in the Aladdin's Cave in the loft of the cottage had the potential for producing more than £70 million worth of the drug. They also had the means to produce synthetic cocaine and LSD. At the moment of the raid, the Crown claimed, Merks was waiting to take the first consignment of the drug in powder form back to Amsterdam to their financial backers.

A full bench of five High Court judges was required when the three men appealed, as their plea that the trial had been prejudiced by publicity had already been heard by three judges. Their sole ground of appeal was that the bench of three judges had erred in refusing to abandon the trial. The publicity, they claimed, had prejudiced a fair and impartial trial.

Mr Daiches, for Stuurman, said the three judges gave an incorrect interpretation of the law. They held that no case of oppression by the Lord Advocate had been established to prevent the trial going on. But the test, he claimed, was not one of oppression. The test was whether what was said was 'so prejudicial to the proper administration of justice in Scotland that the court would entertain the gravest doubt whether a fair and impartial trial was possible, however carefully the trial judge directed the jury.' The Lord Advocate was speaking with two voices, Mr Daiches argued, in saying that although there was a risk of prejudice it was not so grave that a direction by the trial judge could reasonably be expected to remove it.

The appeal court rejected their applications for leave to appeal. Lord Emslie, the Lord Justice General, who presided, rejected their pleas that the pre-trial publicity caused prejudice. The publications occurred almost four months before the trial and, in considering the effect of these publications at the date of the trial, the court was well entitled to bear in mind that the public memory of newspaper articles and news broadcasts and of their detailed contents was 'notoriously short'.

The laboratory equipment used by the drugs ring later made a major contribution to the fight against crime by Lothian and Borders Police. All of the equipment seized in the raid was handed over to the force by the trial judge, Chief Constable Sir John Orr said later that some of the equipment, including a microcomputer and scientific apparatus, was used in the laboratory of the identification branch and to start a toxology service in the force.

As a result, Edinburgh University agreed to integrate their departments of forensic medicine and pathology and to end their work in the field of toxology. (A toxology service is indispensable in the investigation of unexplained and suspicious deaths where blood and urine must be examined for signs of alcohol, drugs and poisons.) Previously, the toxology service for the Crown in Scotland had been rather fragmented. Consequently, the Chief Constable felt the police themselves should have experts for the scientific investigation of crime. And so the activities of the Dutch syndicate, unlike many crimes, did have some benefit for the public good.

CHAPTER 4
J.C. and his Disciples

The antics of the zany managing director of a Glasgow company, Maurice 'Big Jim' Cochrane, known as 'J.C.', rocked the city's normally staid business community and provoked gales of laughter in the drab setting of Glasgow Sheriff Court as he and one of his 'Disciples' were tried for corruption, fraud and attempted fraud.

The evidence presented at their trial might have been scripted by Spike Milligan himself. The jury heard of strange goings-on at the Rotary Tool Co. Ltd, where Cochrane used a large toy elephant as 'a lie detector' in his fur-lined office. He also had a life-size Chinese clay idol, called Bung Ho, as well as a large teddy bear which he used to cuddle as he interviewed people for jobs. Just outside his office was a fully-equipped kitchen where expensive lunches were cooked for him.

The jury also heard of the night a National Coal Board official spent with the oddly-named Anna Grunt, a buxom, blonde, free-lance model from Warsaw, and of the lavish party Cochrane threw at a cost of £47,000, attended by 4,200 people, after he opened a new factory which only cost £26,000.

There were tales of bribes secreted in cigar boxes, wild parties for businessmen at the Crazy Daisy Discotheque in Sauchiehall Street and attempts at the wholesale bribery of the representatives of other companies and officials of nationalised industries with sex, gifts and money.

Flamboyant Cochrane, born in the East End of London, enjoyed a chequered career. He worked as a navvy, an actor and a film cameraman and was even the assistant director of a play starring Sir Laurence Olivier. Later he was a deep-sea fisherman but, in his own words, most of the time he was a con-man and a thief. In 1958 he was jailed for four years for housebreaking offences committed in 1953, having spent the intervening years on the run.

Earlier he had been in the Irish Guards but was discharged because of psychiatric illness. He was 40 when he left prison and was determined to start life anew. He felt absolutely no guilt about his 'second life' as a businessman and thought he was simply part of the British system of commerce. He believed everyone had his price and suddenly found himself in the rat race, bribing and corrupting as he went.

Cochrane's trial outraged and intrigued all Scotland for five weeks as newspapers devoted pages to the lurid escapades of Cochrane with headlines such as 'J.C. — Superstar', 'Bribes, Sex and Porn' and 'Dinner Then Crumpet for Afters'.

In 1965, after a reasonably successful spell as a salesman in Herefordshire, Cochrane started Rotary Tools with Robert Taylor, renting a small shop for £6 a week in Dumbarton Road, Glasgow. Their only staff was a part-time office girl. Cochrane and Taylor became agents for a German firm manufacturing expensive high-quality tools. The business expanded and they moved to bigger premises in Brown Street.

In 1971, Rotary Tools was taken over by Thistle Holdings of Edinburgh. By then Cochrane and Taylor were doing £250,000 of business a year. The chairman of Thistle was the Hon. John Warrender and Cochrane was proud to be associated with an 'hon'. But his downfall began in 1974 when a 38-year-old former salesman, 'Bernie the Bolt' Boyle, gave a statement to his solicitor which started a full-scale police investigation into Rotary Tools.

The investigation into the 'House of Corruption', as it was later called, ended with Cochrane, as the former managing director, and his sales director, 38-year-old James Drysdale, facing 13 charges of corruption, fraud and attempted fraud. They were accused, under the Prevention of Corruption Act, of providing businessmen with the services of women at the Excelsior Hotel at Glasgow Airport and of giving bribes in return for business favours.

The firms involved were: the National Coal Board; the Chrysler Corporation at Linwood, Renfrewshire; two shipbuilding firms, Scotts of Greenock and Lithgows of Port Glasgow; the South of Scotland Electricity Board; and two Ross and Cromarty companies, Highland Fabricators of Nigg Bay and Euronorth Ltd of Evanton.

Cochrane faced additional charges of attempted fraud involving £12,500. It was alleged that he sent the National Coal

Board at Rotherham an account for £8,375 for seven compressed air hoists and seven air trolleys when they had only ordered one of each, and that he sent International Combustion Ltd of Derby an account for £4,124 for ten saws and 60 blades when they had ordered only one saw and six blades. He was also accused of rigging a beauty contest so that his secretary, Carolyn Schultz — later to be his wife — would win.

And there was astonishing allegations of how the engineering company went out to get contracts using sex, bribes and pornography.

The trial began in Glasgow Sheriff Court in May 1976 before Sheriff Stewart Bell. The first witness, Peter Phillips, who was by then chairman of his own company, said he had worked for Rotary Tools for a period of four months in 1971. He was supposed to be sales manager but was, in fact, a salesman. During his short stay with the company he was promoted three times and resigned three times.

Mr Phillips' conflict with Cochrane began on one occasion when they were chasing a substantial order. Phillips felt the client would eventually place the order because he knew the equipment was good. But this was not good enough for Cochrane, who wanted things to move more quickly. He suggested that Cochrane could use a number of different methods, adding 'All men are bent. You are bent.'

When Phillips replied 'Oh no I'm not', Cochrane said: 'All men are and we will exploit that. You will find that man's weakness whatever it is.'

Mr Phillips told the court:

> I asked what he meant and he said a man might want a woman or money or perhaps it was pornography he might be interested in. I think at that time a series of leaflets were produced describing pornographic things. I was given one of them to show to the client but I refused. Cochrane thought it was highly amusing to have this attitude in the world as it is today.

A week later Phillips resigned. However, when Cochrane offered him a promotion he decided to stay on as he had no other job to go to. He was to resign on two more occasions.

Phillips recalled a conversation with Drysdale, his immediate boss, in which Drysdale virtually repeated Cochrane's remarks about methods of obtaining orders:

> I told him there were no circumstances where I would take that action and, besides, I felt it left the company open to all manner of things. I asked what would happen if one of those individuals were to talk and he said it would be a relatively simple matter to arrange for this man to meet with some kind of argument in a pub and for him to be sorted out.

Phillips said he was paid £3,000 a year plus commission and a car but he was not a very successful salesman. He denied that he was fired and said he was not prepared to use the methods advocated by his employer. Cochrane was a man of unusual habits and an odd sense of humour.

Asked if his jaw dropped when Cochrane showed him pornography, Phillips said, 'It was not pornography that made my jaw drop, it was the way I was expected to use it.' He had seen pornography before but never used as a sales aid. He was told the man he was selling to was bent and that his particular fancy was pornography. He was to take him some and show it to him. Instead he tore up the material and threw it away.

Mr Phillips concluded his evidence by saying, 'I can say categorically that I will never ever forget Rotary Tools. Never.'

Rotary's former financial controller, Charles Neville, described Cochrane's office as 'bizarre'. The walls were covered with imitation fur wallpaper and decorated with swords and spears. Cochrane's behaviour was also bizarre. He was the type of man who fired memos right, left and centre and it was not uncommon for staff to last only a day or two.

Neville was appointed financial controller in 1972 and later became a director. He was aware that payments were made to salesmen to obtain orders. But the methods explained to him by Cochrane involved more than just money. The policy of the company was 'to entertain'.

Cochrane told him that, if necessary, payment would be made to a buyer or whoever was in a position to place orders. Neville was not surprised that this was done but he was surprised at the extent. As financial controller, he gave money to salesmen for the purpose of paying officials of other companies. The money was normally entered as 'expenses' or 'entertainment' in the books.

Payments probably totalling £300 were made to Christopher Meechan of Scott's shipyard. Walter Renfrew of Scott's also received various payments. On one occasion, a cigar was removed from a cigar box and £50 or £60 put in the resulting space. Josiah Silcock of the South of Scotland Electricity Board at Kincardine probably received over £300 and Robert McKay of Chrysler Scotland between £500 and £600. In some cases, people were receiving five per cent of the business obtained. On one occasion, Neville handed an envelope containing £50 to McKay, who was in a position to give orders for tool and spare parts.

John Docherty of Vosper Thorneycroft of Southampton was paid £50 on at least two occasions and Desmond Dixon of Darchem Engineering Co. of Stockton-on-Tees, Rotary's biggest customer, received payments totalling £2,000 over a period of two years. Individual payments to him were as much as £500.

Neville revealed that girls were hired from escort agencies to provide drinks at parties in Rotary's premises. He recalled being in Cochrane's office with three customers and a girl called Anna Lanska. There was another girl he did not know and a third girl was expected. He saw Cochrane give each of the girls £25. They were to be escorts for the evening.

When police started their investigation in May 1974, Cochrane instructed Neville to go through the company records to make sure they contained nothing incriminating. He destroyed a few petty cash slips.

Mr Neville also described for the court memos issued by Cochrane to him and their staff. In one he told Neville, 'The only union I believe in is me.' In another he talked of a sealed envelope which gave advice on his succession in the event of his demise.

Neville stated that a record of payments made to obtain business was kept in a special 'bung book', on the suggestion of the auditors. The book was introduced to protect directors from any allegations by their parent company that they were pocketing the money themselves.

A mammoth party was thrown by Cochrane in August 1973 to mark the opening of the company's new premises. The famous jazz trumpeter, Dizzy Gillespie, was brought in from Brussels and pianist Ray Ellington was also there to entertain Cochrane's 4,000 guests. The cost was never determined but Neville thought they spent more than £15,000.

Neville also recalled a party to celebrate Cochrane's departure to Russia on a sales trip. In attendance were people in Russian costumes, university students who sang in Russian and a stripper.

Despite such merriment, there was an aura of fear in the company. Cochrane was a violent man whom Neville had seen throw ashtrays and waste paper baskets at people.

Rotary broke into the lucrative Clyde shipyard market by giving backhanders to certain influential employees. According to the company's 'Mr Fixit' — Bernard Boyle, their top salesman — the yards involved were Scotts and Lithgows. Among the perks offered, he claimed, were a cigar box containing cash, a refrigerator, gramophone records, fishing equipment, expensive party invitations and five per cent commission on orders gained by Rotary through an employee's influence.

Mr Boyle testified that he had joined the company in January 1972, later becoming general manager. Shortly after he joined, Cochrane told him that one method of overcoming resistance to sales would be to 'bend'. Cochrane's theory was that every man had his price and this could be money, gifts or women.

The firm was having trouble getting orders from the two shipyards and it was felt that inducements should be offered to key people. Boyle's initial contact was with a storeman at Scotts, Christopher Meechan.

He invited Mr Meechan to a Rotary party in 1972, after which Rotary were reasonably successful with Scotts. After discovering that Meechan was interested in fishing, Boyle was given money by Cochrane to buy fishing equipment for him.

He was told to tell Meechan he would get five per cent of any future orders he gave Rotary. The first payment of £20 was made six weeks after the first order. On another occasion Meechan received a sum nearer £100. Boyle estimated that in total Meechan was given three or four hundred pounds.

In 1973, it was thought that payment should also be made to Meechan's boss, Walter Renfrew, the plant engineer. There was some worry that if it came out that Meechan was getting money while his senior was not there would have been no more orders. Nevertheless, Boyle took Renfrew to a boxing match in the Albany Hotel, Glasgow and gave him a box of cigars. Cochrane had exchanged one of the cigars for a wad of notes amounting, Boyle believed, to about £100.

Boyle then told the court how he was ordered to buy gramophone records costing between £15 and £18 for Robert Goodwin, the chief buyer at Lithgows, who was interested in chamber music. Mr Goodwin accepted the records without comment and put them in his drawer. He mentioned he had a faulty fridge made by the same company as Rotary's air tools and asked whether it would be possible to get him a spare part. Cochrane thought this would be an ideal opportunity to give him a new fridge but Goodwin did not really want two fridges. When asked what else he would like, Goodwin said he did not have a colour TV set. Some time later, Boyle saw a music centre at Rotary premises and was told, 'That's for Mr Goodwin.' Shortly afterwards they got their first order from Lithgows – six small hand grinds, worth £110 each.

In 1973, Rotary staged the Miss Airpower Beauty competition with prizes of a case of whisky, a magnum of champagne, a pair of fashion shoes and a dress – all donated by Strathclyde companies. On the night of the event, Boyle went to Glasgow Airport to meet Miss United Kingdom, Veronica Cross, who was one of the judges. Cochrane had ordered him to tell Miss Cross there was to be only one winner and that was to be Carolyn Schultz, Cochrane's secretary. Cross didn't appear to be upset or bothered about it.

Mr Boyle said he resigned in January 1974. Cochrane wanted him to work 80 to 100 hours a week, not only in the office but out in the field and even at Cochrane's own home. After he resigned he received two telephone calls asking him to come back.

When he went into Cochrane's office to collect his insurance cards, Cochrane locked the door after him. Drysdale and Neville were also present. Then followed what Boyle described as 'one and a half hours of terror with threats of physical violence by Cochrane.'

Cochrane told him, 'Nobody leaves Rotary Tools,' and that if he dared reveal to anyone, including the police, what was happening, he would be a sorry man. 'He was raving about the office,' Boyle recounted, 'throwing his jacket off and continually coming over and threatening to strike me.'

The stream of abuse and threats continued until Cochrane eventually tired of 'his little game' and Boyle was allowed to leave.

Afterwards, Boyle went to his lawyer, who took a statement from him about Rotary Tools. Three or four weeks later, the police called at his home to interview him. He denied he was sacked because he had become 'a problem child.'

Mr Goodwin, who said he was an organist and very interested in music, admitted receiving six classical LP's after a conversation with Cochrane about music, but testified that he had refused to accept an £86 music centre. To have taken such a gift, he felt would have been unethical. It was part of his duties to place orders, he said, but he had not regarded the gifts as bribes or sinister in any way.

The records were delivered by a salesman who said, 'Here's a present from Mr Cochrane.' Goodwin accepted them as a goodwill gift. Later Cochrane phoned to say he was sending him something. When he got home he found the music centre with the price shown as £86. He had never accepted gifts of that magnitude from anyone and called Cochrane to ask him to take it back. Cochrane asked him if he would take something smaller such as a cassette recorder and he agreed.

When Cochrane phoned him later to ask if he wanted a television set, Goodwin told him he was not interested and nothing more was said. He would never accept a bribe, Goodwin told the court. If he had thought there was anything sinister in Cochrane's gift-giving he would have gone to his managing director. It never entered his head that it could put him in a compromising situation.

A 22-year-old model, Maretta Barnsley, told the court that she came to Scotland in 1973 to visit relatives and joined the Cosmopolitan Agency to work as a model. The agency used to send girls to parties at Rotary Tools to act as hostesses. She attended two parties. After the second one, she got a phone call from Cochrane, who invited her to join him and some other people at the Crazy Daisy disco the following night.

When she arrived, she met a girl called Anna, who spoke with a foreign accent, and another girl. Cochrane, his secretary and other employees were there, along with three men from the North of Scotland who, she understood, were potential customers.

After a meal and some drinks, the three girls and the three men were taken to the Excelsior Hotel and had more drinks in a bedroom booked in advance. Afterwards the couples split up. Barnsley remained in the bedroom with a middle-aged man and spent the night with him. She had been paid £30 by Cochrane and realised there would be more expected of her than the general entertaining duties of a hostess.

Anna Grunt, a 25-year-old freelance model who worked for the agency under the name Anna Lanska, said she was given £6 to attend a Rotary party to sell drinks and look after customers. A dozen girls were hired from various agencies and Cochrane briefed them on what they should do and how nice they should be to customers. They were later taken to the Excelsior Hotel, where she spent the night with a middle-aged man she identified when he was brought into court. The next day, she was given £35 by Cochrane. She slept with another Rotary customer later and was paid the same fee.

John Sim, a 51-year-old production controller with the National Coal Board, shamefacedly admitted he was the man who spent the night with Anna. While he was having a meal at the Excelsior Hotel with a Rotary salesman, a girl with a mid-European or Polish accent came in and joined them. The salesman introduced them and suggested that since he had to stay in Glasgow, he might as well use a room in the hotel booked by Rotary.

'It became obvious during the meal that the girl and I were going to the room together. She said she wanted to go up with me and I accepted the offer.'

They spent the night together and next morning he dropped her off in Glasgow. He denied he was in a position to place orders for Rotary and denied any approach was made to him after the night with Anna. Even if he had been given thousands of pounds and free holidays he could not have helped Rotary.

Mr Sim denied before the court that, having missed all the famous Rotary parties, he had asked for a private party on his own. He also denied that he wanted 'a red-hot night on the town' at someone else's expense. Sim said he was in Glasgow to give an address at Strathclyde University to the Mining Institute of Scotland, of which he was president. He agreed that the night with the model was 'a momentary one-off situation.'

Mrs Catherine Beattie, the wife of comedian Johnny Beattie, who owned the Kitty Lamont Model Agency, testified that she was asked to provide girls for the beauty contest and also to be a judge. She also provided the compère, Arthur Montford, the sports broadcaster. Cochrane, she said, told her, 'I am perfectly prepared to have you as a judge provided you understand that Miss Schultz, my secretary, wins the prize.'

'I said how could he be sure she would be the best-looking person there. I thought she was an extremely pretty girl and the type who would win a beauty competition but I had not seen the other competitors.'

Cochrane also told her he was already having one of the prizes, a model gown, made in Schultz's size. Backstage at the contest, Schultz came forward and said: 'Don't forget I have to win this. We have already taken the prizes home with us.' Mrs Beattie added:

'It was no contest. They were all very ordinary. Miss Schultz was the best-looking there. I was very angry at the time and I can assure you if there had been anyone better looking than Miss Schultz, it would have given me the greatest pleasure to have chosen her.'

She decided to close Cochrane's account as he was not the sort of person she wanted to deal with. She sent a bill to Cochrane a week later and received a nasty letter in reply. She decided she would rather pay the girls herself than have to deal with Rotary Tools again.

Mr Neville's wife, Helen, told the court she was forced to enter the beauty contest. Her husband told her on the night before the contest that she had to enter, on the boss's orders. She was neither willing nor unwilling to enter but if she had not she knew it was her husband who would have suffered.

Mr Montford said Miss Schultz was a clear-cut winner in the beauty contest.

Mrs Ann Cameron, who owned the Cosmopolitan Agency, said she provided girls for promotional work but she took them away from a Rotary party because they were sitting round drinking and no promotional work seemed to be taking place.

The courtroom rocked with laughter when Andrew Lyall, who was Rotary's senior sales executive, gave evidence. He handled the company's Coal Board account and knew Mr Sim. Lyall testified that when Sim mentioned he was coming to Glasgow in November 1973 to give a lecture he arranged to meet him for a meal and a drink. When informed of this arrangement Cochrane said he would send female company, mentioning Anna Lanska. The coal board account with Rotary was worth about £20,000 a year, Lyall explained, but Sim was not in a position to influence orders. Cochrane was probably unaware of that.

Lyall said that in his dealings with the Coal Board he had to entertain everyone at a colliery from pitboy to the top man. Sometimes he took workers for a cup of tea and a scone in the canteen. But when one reached the post of production manager it was the Excelsior.

But cross-examined by Cochrane's solicitor, J. Ross Harper, one of Scotland's leading criminal lawyers and later President of the Law Society of Scotland, Lyall denied it was suggested to Cochrane that Sim wanted a woman.

Mr Harper said: 'I suggest to you that as far as Mr Sim was concerned, it was not a cup of tea and a scone in the canteen. It was Miss Lanska at the Excelsior ... It was crumpet for Sim. That was more his style, because he asked for it, didn't he?'

Lyall denied this, but Mr Harper continued: 'When this beautiful but albeit skinny blonde sat down at your table, did Mr Sim and Miss Lanska seem to be getting on well? Did she call him sweetie?'

Lyall replied he did not know.

'But they certainly were getting on well enough for you to leave before the meat course. Did Mr Sim rub his hands and give you a big wink? What this à la carte or table d'hôte or was it all inclusive . . . an omelette surprise?'

After the loud laughter subsided, Harper added, 'It's all a bit farcical, isn't it, Mr Lyall? And I have to suggest to you that Mr Sim knew what was for afters.'

Donald Green, who joined Rotary as general manager in 1972 testified that Cochrane was quite ruthless and exerted control through fear. On one occasion Green was told to fire quite a number of people to get authority. Cochrane said the way to get authority was to inculcate fear.

Green stated that Cochrane's nickname was 'J.C.', their order book was 'The Bible'. The company premises were called 'The Church' and the salesmen were referred to as 'The Disciples.'

He recalled how on one occasion he was called to Cochrane's home with two other employees at 11.30 a.m. Cochrane was in bed with his secretary. Cochrane said he wanted to see his face. After five weeks with the firm, he was sacked without any reason being given.

Mr Harper asked him, 'Did you think Cochrane suffered from a kind of megalomania?'

Green replied: 'That was the word that was in my mind. I was just going to say that. Also paranoia. First there was the ostentatious decor of his room, then the way he handled staff, firing at will and the verbal butchering of them and then the odd moments of compassion.'

The hilarity in court continued as another former salesman, Alexander Drennan, recounted the zany exploits of his boss. To anyone who did not know Chochrane they would have thought was was completely mad, he said.

'He used to throw projectiles at me across the room when I was in the office. He threw an oil lamp in my direction and he also had some bakelite eggs which he threw at me. It was funny because he never hit me.'

Once he saw Cochrane interviewing a young girl for a job as a clerkess. He told her to sit on a toy elephant in his office and said it was a lie detector and that the eyes would flash if she told a lie. The young lady duly obliged.

'This was a young girl he had never met in his life and he made her sit on this elephant. He had spotlights on the roof of the office controlled by switches under his desk. When she gave an answer he would switch on the spotlights which gave the appearance of the elephant's eyes lighting up.'

Cochrane told the girl, 'You are not telling the truth' and occasionally she would admit it.

Asked if he had ever seen Cochrane conducting an interview while cuddling a teddy bear, Mr Drennan said:

> No, but I have seen him sit in with applicants for jobs pretending he was also an applicant. He would moan about being kept waiting for so long and then say rude things about the boss of the firm who, of course, was him. He once pretended to be applying for a job as a cleaner.

Asked if he had ever seen Cochrane do anything zany, he replied:

> I once received a memo from him instructing me to marry an office girl I hardly knew. You can take it from me it was a direct order and although I didn't carry it out, Cochrane would have pressed ahead if he had thought he would have got away with it. You can be sure of that.

Mr Drennan told the court that in his dealings with the South of Scotland Electricity Board he gave Mr Josiah Silcock envelopes containing cash four or five times over a period of 18 months. It was hard to say whether the payments helped orders as they had been doing reasonably well with them. Mr Silcock kept pressing him for meals and used to say: 'What about all these bottles of whisky being handed round? How about one for me.' Drennan was given money to give to him.

In April 1974, Cochrane told him there was the possibility of an investigation by the Fraud Squad. He told him to tell Silcock what was happening and not to have a heart attack when the police arrived at his door.

Mr Silcock, a 64-year-old stores clerk at Kincardine Power Station for ten years until he was sacked in 1974, admitted Drennan gave him money. Drennan told him, he stated, that he could do himself a lot of good by accepting money. He asked Drennan if he was trying to bribe him and the salesman just laughed and said it would be just a gift from his expenses.

Silcock forgot about it until he was going on holiday, when Drennan again raised the subject, saying the money would help with his holiday. He foolishly accepted an envelope containing £85. Later he was given an envelope containing £120 by Cochrane. The total he received was £430.

'I took it to be a goodwill gift. I was never asked to do anything for it. I was never in a position to influence orders. I've lost ten years pension, a good job and my health. I was dismissed without pay.'

Marilyn Sheritt, a clerk, said she was sent a memo by Cochrane instructing her to marry a salesman. She took it as a joke and kept it as a memento of Cochrane's unusual sense of humour. She told the court Cochrane ordered her to alter the figures in orders for the National Coal Board and International Combustion Ltd. She believed this was done to improve the company's cash flow.

Walter Renfrew, the 55-year-old plant manager at Scotts shipyard, spoke of receiving boxes of cigars with money hidden inside. He had known Cochrane when he was a traveller and met him again in 1972. In January 1973, he attended a boxing match with Cochrane at the Albany Hotel in Glasgow; Cochrane drove him home and handed him a box of cigars.

Two weeks later, Bernard Boyle handed him a wrapped box at the shipyard. It was another box of cigars but he put it in a cupboard without opening it. Some months later, the police called and asked him to open the box. Inside was £50 in £5 notes.

In August 1973, after a meal with Drysdale at the Malmaison Restaurant he was given a tin wrapped in brown paper. He knew it was a gift.

'This concerned me because of my principles and I went to see my director and asked 'What does one do?' I was told it was normal business practice to accept small gifts provided it did not cloud my judgment.'

He took the tin of cigars to work next day because he did not smoke and put them in his bottom drawer. Three weeks later, during a function at the plant he opened the tin to give the lads in the shop a cigar. Inside he found £60.

'I was annoyed sick and was bewildered what to do with it. I gave the money away to various charities, including Christian Aid and the Salvation Army.'

Earlier, he had tried to give the money back to Boyle, who

had called late one night at his home with a bottle of whisky. Boyle told him it would virtually mean the sack for him if he took the money back. It was a mystery why he had been given money, as he had never had any pressure for orders put on him by anyone at Rotary Tools.

Asked why Cochrane would want to give him cigars and money and invite him for meals and to boxing matches, Mr Renfrew said he was interested in Cochrane's attitude to life. He found it interesting talking to him. Cochrane reciprocated and gave him a book and wrote on the flyleaf, 'To Walter with affection regards J.C.'

Christopher Meechan, who also lost his job with Scotts, said Boyle took him to see Cochrane, who told him, 'You never had a handshake like this in your life.' When he withdrew his hand he was holding about £50. He was not in a position to get Rotary an order but Boyle suggested he would get five per cent of any business. He agreed he was more or less talked into it by a fast-talking salesman.

Desmond Dixon, a 52-year-old former chief buyer at Darchem Engineering, admitted receiving £500 in registered envelopes from Cochrane but said the money was not for passing fake orders but for recommending Rotary to other firms. He denied being sent several payments of £500 and receiving a total of £3,000.

One of the charges against Cochrane and Drysdale was that they had offered Dixon a holiday in Blackpool or Liverpool as an inducement or a reward for showing favour to Rotary. Dixon told the court that his company had in fact never placed orders with Rotary. He did accept, however, that 10 invoices he had passed for payment, supposedly placed with Rotary, had false order numbers and were not accompanied by a 'Goods Received' note. The only explanation he could offer was that he had been extremely overworked.

Kenneth Park, the chief accountant with Darchem, described finding in 1973, 10 invoices in Dixon's handwriting related to orders worth thousands of pounds which appeared to have been placed with Rotary. But there was no record of the goods having been received. Payments were made on all these invoices.

Another Rotary salesman, William Sherlock, recalled going

on a business trip with Cochrane, who arranged to take two girls to a hotel in the New Forest. They arranged to have a meal served in Cochrane's room. Cochrane asked the waitress if she was Norwegian or Swedish and she told him she was Finnish.

"He asked if she did massage and when she said 'Yes' Cochrane said, 'Oh. I'll have one later.'"

Cochrane's behaviour in the hotel was unusual. He ordered endless pots of tea. He was a flamboyant characer and a bit Bohemian in his ways. Cochrane had treated him well, sent Christmas cards to his children and once advanced him £300 when he was going through a bad patch.

The court was then told of the night in November 1973 when three businessmen were flown from Inverness to Glasgow in a chartered aircraft and, after meeting Cochrane, were taken to the Crazy Daisy disco. There was a party of about 15 and the three businessmen were paired off with three girls. Slightly-built, bespectacled, Angus Cuthbertson, managing director of Euronorth Ltd, and his sales director, John McLean, were accompanied by Vincent Doherty of Highland Fabrications Ltd.

Mr McLean testified that, after a meal when they asked Cochrane where they were to stay the night, they were told they would be going to the Excelsior Hotel. Cars were arranged and the girls went with them. McLean said he was with Maretta Barnsley but denied he had asked for 'talent' to be laid on.

Mr Cuthbertson said they were taken to Rotary's premises. He was taken aback by the office. It was dimly lit and there skins on the wall. Music was being played in the background. They were given refreshments and shown round the warehouse but from the stock he saw his firm could not do business with Rotary.

> I did not like the atmosphere. We were told to sit on a settee. Two young ladies came in and were told to sit beside us. Photographs were taken which I did not very much approve of.
>
> Then there was one incident which put me right off. One of the salesman said something to Cochrane. He picked up a butane gas cylinder which he was using as an emergency lamp on his desk and hurled it at the salesman. The thing exploded and gas escaped into the office. It was not very businesslike. At one point, Cochrane got on to an exercise bike and talked to us while he was exercising.

At the Crazy Daisy, Cochrane took charge of the seating arrangements, telling McLean to sit beside the two girls who had been at the office. Later, a third girl, Jennifer McGregor, came in and spoke to Cochrane and then sat down beside him. Absolutely no business was done.

Cuthbertson was very unhappy about the whole night because the band and the singer were very noisy and they could not hear themselves speak. Cochrane seemed to sense he was not enjoying it and he threw over a table with all the drinks on it, saying 'Let's put some life into this.'

The three of them were paired off with the girls and when they arrived at the hotel they found they had each been booked into a room as Mr and Mrs.

After drinks, Jennifer McGregor phoned her babysitter and asked Cuthbertson if it would be all right if she went home. He gave her £1 for a taxi and after seeing her off, went to his room. Next morning, seeing no sign of McLean or Doherty at breakfast, he went to their rooms. He saw the two women with them. The woman with Doherty spoke with a foreign accent.

The court was told that Mr Doherty had since left the country.

Robert McKay, the former chief buyer at the Chrysler plant at Linwood, Renfrewshire, denied he had demanded money to influence business. He admitted receiving about £400 from Cochrane over a period of four years. He knew he was doing wrong. He had not told anyone about the money, not even his wife.

When he was asked if he was known as 'Mr Five Per Cent' there was loud laughter from the public benches as he replied: 'That was a title given to many buyers in industry. It is a jocular remark – just as lawyers are all supposed to be shysters.'

McKay had visited Cochrane at his office 12 to 15 times and was given money. He assumed it was in lieu of entertainments, as Cochrane never took him out for meals. He had been in a position to give Rotary business but he had never regarded the payments as bribes.

William Chalmers, managing director of Thistle Industrial Holdings, said his firm bought a 51 per cent controlling interest in Rotary in December 1971. The agreement was that if the aggregate profit of Rotary exceeded £90,000 by 31

December 1973, Thistle would pay an extra £1 a share on the shares already purchased, including those of Cochrane. The agreement also stated that if profits exceeded £135,000 the shareholders would get another £3 a share. In addition, Cochrane was given a profit-sharing arrangement of four per cent of the profits each year if they were in excess of £30,000.

The accounts finally submitted showed that profits exceeded £135,000 and Cochrane stood to gain an extra £6,300 for his shares and £2,000 from his four per cent agreement. During investigations, however, it was found that the accounts up to March 1974 in fact showed a loss of £125,000.

Fifty-one-year-old Cochrane was often in tears as he told the court of his spectacular rise and fall in the world of big business. But he still brought a laugh when he said he was now selling knickers and nighties in open-air markets. He enjoyed it, he said, because people did not speak with 'forked tongues'.

His voice was filled with emotion as he told his solicitor, Mr Harper, of Rotary's beginnings in a £6 a week rented office. He said he had been called James for 25 years as he thought his name Maurice was 'effete, cissy.' He was also known as 'J.C.'

Asked who was responsible for the administration of Rotary, Cochrane broke down as he said, 'I was basically responsible.'

At the time of the takeover, Cochrane explained, the administrative side was 'a bit hairy.' He had no experience of accountancy and just used common sense. He was enthusiastic more than anything else and he lived for his work.

The hardest part was controlling salesmen. 'You have to be a hard and shrewd cookie to control a sales force. You never know where you are with them. I tried to be tough, humorous and fair without being nasty. I found it a bit of a strain.'

He enjoyed the creative side of building up a business. It might sound ridiculous he said, but money did not mean much to him. He gave most of his money away.

'But there were many things I didn't enjoy. I don't think you have to be a rat to be in the rat race. I fought desperately trying not to be one.' He denied he was going to make 'a quick killing' on his shares after the takeover.

He told the court about his unusual office and his Monty Python-Spike Milligan sense of humour. Like Cyril Fletcher, he wrote rather sick odes. In his office there were a couple of spears and fur wallpaper. He later got a stuffed elephant from Harrods.

'I didn't want it to be left there over Christmas. All the monkeys and giraffes had been sold.' He later got another smaller elephant called 'Ellie' which he used as a lie detector as a joke.

The eight-foot high Bung Ho idol in his office was also just a joke. At sales meetings, the odd salesman who said he was having trouble getting to see someone was told 'to kneel in front of Bung Ho and he would tell him whether to give a bottle of whisky or lunch or what.'

Cochrane told the court he had not made a fortune and had not stashed money away in Zurich. He denied there was an aura of violence at Rotary and said that although people had started to make 'clucking noises' in their direction, allegations of widespread corruption were untrue. Out of 1,500 or 2,000 customers, he said, gifts had only been given to nine or ten.

'It was a thing we hated and deplored but we were in the system and a lot of people who have come to this court have told lies about it. There are men of substance who not only demand bottles of whisky but specify the brand they want.'

The first payments were made to Chrysler and their chief buyer, Mr McKay. McKay made it clear he wanted not lunches particularly, nor whisky, but five per cent. Refusing to give it, Cochrane claimed, would have meant the loss of a lot of business from Chrysler and from other people. The word would have got around.

Cochrane said everyone knew about the bung book, including the auditors, the chairman of Thistle and the staff at Rotary. At one time, the Hon. James Warrender, asked him, 'James. If anything should ever go wrong with this bung book, would it ever fall in my lap?' Cochrane replied that it certainly would.

Cochrane stated that on one occasion a salesman told him he had an old friend who was a senior official at the National Coal Board coming to see him and asked him to find a girl for him. Cochrane had never met Mr Sim and did not even know his name until he saw it on the indictment. Although he had paid Anna Grunt £35 to entertain Sim he did not provide girls 'willy-nilly' for customers' whims. He had only two requests to provide girls and the court had heard of these.

He also denied any knowledge of his salesman, Boyle, paying £400 to Mr Meechan but admitted giving Mr Goodwin records and a cassette recorder after sensing he wanted 'sweetening'. But money paid to John Docherty of Vosper Thorneycroft was for legitimate services.

There was frequent laughter in the court as Cochrane described the giant party he threw to celebrate the opening of new premises.

'It was all free. We supplied food and drink. We knocked a wall down but it wasn't exactly a Jericho – we knocked it down and built it back up again later. We knocked down the wall because we could not have got all the people in if we hadn't. Everyone was there – John Doe and his neighbours.

We had belly dancers we said came from Persia but actually they came from Whitechapel Road, London. We said the lighting was by Alfredo Durante but we made up the name and we did it ourselves.

It was a bit of a Barnum and Bailey. I enjoyed it more than selling air tools. I wish we could have had one very month. We spent £400 to hire a piano and £3,000 on special lighting. The whole place was transformed.

We had lots of portaloos and the St John ambulancemen and I paid the police – and that must not be taken sinisterly. The police were paid to be there just like at a football match.

We had Securicor there and my company doctor found them loading my whisky into their van. I think the News of the World reporter counted three or four thousand empty bottles after the party.'

Asked about the cost, Cochrane replied, 'I couldn't quantify it. Over £20,000 I would think.'

He said he had tried to book Humphrey Lyttelton but he liked watching birds – the feathered type – and thought that ornithologising in Pembrokeshire was preferable to the party. And so they had Ray Ellington and Dizzy Gillespie instead.

He had 20 pipers march in at 5.30 a.m. playing the lament 'The Flowers of the Forest.' 'It was very moving. It was a beautiful sight as dawn broke over Glasgow to see these pipers coming down the road.'

He asked every woman on his staff to enter the beauty contest and promised them a free hairdo and the afternoon off. It was only for a laugh that he said he had spent the first prize.

Asked if it was a fraudulent scheme to get the prizes he said: 'No. My wife is very hurt by this charge. She has suffered a lot. She is a good girl, well-bred and well educated. She is a beautiful woman.'

He denied giving instructions that his secretary had to win the beauty contest. She was a beautiful woman and won on merit, he said. He would have been proud of her if she had been last.

He admitted, however, inflating a £1,000 invoice to the National Coal Board to £8,000. It was sent to a firm of debt collectors to help increase Rotary's cash flow. The same was done to International Combustion when their invoice was increased from £400 to £4,000. Later credit notes correcting the 'mistakes' were sent out.

He then told of his long period of ill-health when he became obsessed with his bodily functions. At one stage, he offered Thistle his resignation and wanted to run away to Spain and become a barman.

'Sweeteners' paid to businessmen were 'Happitisers', he said. He had no choice but to provide them.

Cochrane also spoke of the jokes he used to play to shock his staff and brighten things up a bit. On one occasion, he took off his wig and put it on the floor of a posh Paris hotel, standing back to watch elegant ladies stepping over 'this hairy thing.'

Many of Cochrane's staff gave evidence on his behalf. Salesman Robert Thorburn said he was an unusual employer but a good one. He was a generous man and on many occasions had helped staff with financial and domestic problems. He was more like a family counsellor than a boss.

He recalled Cochrane sitting behind his desk, cuddling a giant teddy bear, as he interviewed three salesmen. He spoke to the teddy bear as if it was someone he was getting advice from. Mr Cochrane had invited him to attend in order to watch the reactions of the salesmen.

'They all looked rather blank and amazed and I could appreciate that.'

Austin Harney said Cochrane had a mercurial temperament and was close to genius in business matters. Another former employee said Cochrane was 'hard but fair'. A clerk said the words 'cash bender' was written clearly in the ledger for gifts and gratuities.

An accountant who carried out their audit said Rotary were given a clear certificate despite the fact that there was a lack of suitable documentation on expenses and entertaining. The company's bills for entertaining rose from £5,616 to £16,750 and directors' expenses from £3,970 to £6,340.

Cochrane's attractive young wife, Carolyn, said her husband was a hypochondriac who at one time thought he was dying of cancer. Every time he had a sore throat he used to send for the company doctor to give him an antibiotic. He once instructed her to buy one of every item sold at Boots and used to keep medical volumes in his office. He was sure he had cancer, changing his idea of what kind it was every week. She felt there was nothing physically wrong with him and suggested he should see a psychiatrist, which he eventually did.

But as soon as he left the company, Cochrane's wife explained, there was a miraculous change; his obsessions ceased, although he was still a hypochondriac. He had been delighted at the takeover. He had never mixed with the aristocracy because of his background and felt proud when an 'Honourable' became part of Rotary.

Mr Harper asked Carolyn why, given that she was a former beauty queen and Cochrane a man in his fifties with unusual traits, she had married him. She replied: 'Because I love him. Strange as it may seem he is the most lovable man I have ever met. He is very kind-hearted and a very good man who treated his employees well. That's why I married him.'

She told how on one occasion her husband wanted to shock his general manager, Mr Green. At the time her husband was ill in bed and held meetings at home. He asked her to jump into bed with him to shock Green and she did so, still with her shoes on and her notebook and pencil. When Green came in, her husband started to dictate a letter to her. On another occasion her husband put ice cubes down the trousers of a very staid salesman.

The Hon. John Warrender, chairman of Thistle Holdings (which took over Rotary) denied that his group knew about the cash payments to win contracts. He had no part in the day-today management of Rotary and relied on information from its directors and the auditors. He realised now that the use of improper methods had been kept hidden from Thistle. The eccentric Cochrane had assured him that cash payments had stopped when they had joined 'reputable people.'

Warrender pointed out that Cochrane was not the only bad apple in the barrel, and that if he had been he would not have lasted so long. There were three bad apples – three executives conspiring to keep information away from the group. It was a complete and utter lie, Warrender stated, that he knew before the takeover that cash was being paid in a limited number of cases.

'Do you really think', he asked any sane man would have bought a business like that? You are now suggesting I am insane.'

Mr William Carmichael, prosecuting, pointed out in his closing speech to the jury that one of the exhibits was the Bible. He added, 'If you choose to worship idols, idols like Bung Ho, you could call Rotary Tools the House of Corruption.'

Mr Carmichael dropped seven of the charges against Drysdale, three of them relating to providing women in return for business favours. Three others concerned alleged payments to officials of Chrysler, Vosper Thorneycroft and Dercham. The seventh alleged he had sent out tools sent in for repairs, without the repairs having been carried out and charged the firms concerned.

He also dropped part of a charge against Cochrane alleging he invited firms to donate prizes for the beauty contest and appropriated the prizes by fraud. However, he accused Cochrane of conducting a smear campaign against the Crown witnesses:

> Calling a man a pimp, what has that got to do with the case? Accusing another man of going around the office bothering girls and another two men of being extortionists and another of being a weed and another man of snogging with a woman.
>
> All this business of Cochrane having a crazy sort of humour is to throw you off the scent. But Cochrane is no fool. I tried to examine him and I quite freely admit he got the better of me. He had the answers all there. He was an actor and you may consider his evidence was performance, a very good performance.

But was it the truth? I think Mr Cochrane is a pretty shrewd businessman.

Mr Harper, for Cochrane, said his client had been steering his ship through a potential 'a sea of extortion.' He was unfairly charged with corrupting a number of people in a variety of ways. 'One man's meat is Anna Grunt, another man's meat is tickets to boxing matches and another man's meat is cash.' But was Cochrane a 'mind reader who knows what people want?' Witnesses have indicated they were suddenly provided with what they particularly wanted. Was it coincidence the demands were so perfectly met?

'You remember at Christmas we all used to put our notes up the chimney for Santa and hoped they would not be burned. If Mr Cochrane was not a mind reader, was he perhaps Father Christmas going over the chimneys of Mr Sim, Mr Goodwin, Mr McKay and Mr Renfrew and collecting notes of what they wanted?

Was he directing Miss Grunt to the right happy home as a Christmas present? Perhaps Bung Ho, the idol, had magical powers and was able to tell Mr Cochrane what was wanted by each of these people.'

Mr Harper concluded by saying: 'This case has everything and one wonders sometimes on hearing the evidence whether Mr Cochrane was two men. Was Cochrane the evil man, the head of the House of Corruption or a compassionate man in the rat race? Was he a Jekyll and Hyde employer, shooting off wild memoranda, visiting sick salesmen in hospital and carrying out personal business instead of devoting more time to his work?'

Cochrane, he said, was the last of the big spenders, an old-fashioned millionaire Eartha Kitt would have liked. He was 'a man who went from the nadir of irrepressible boyish humour to the Zenith of building up a business. His humour was not a Damon Runyon act to put the jury off the scent.'

Four more charges against Drysdale were dropped. He was by now only charged with giving a tin of cigars with £60 to Mr Renfrew and money to Mr Silcock for showing favour. Sheriff Bell then told the jury they should acquit Cochrane of providing the services of two girls to officials of the Highland firm. The Sheriff said the law was passed to protect employees and the jury might think that managing directors were well able to look after themselves. If one managing director chose to spend money on another managing director that was up to him.

He told the jury: 'This is not a court of morals. It is not our job to pass moral judgment.'

The five-week trial ended with the jury out for more than five hours. For Big Jim Cochrane the party was over. He was found guilty on eight charges, jailed for a year and fined £650. But Drysdale was cleared of the remaining charges against him and walked free, accusing Thistle of breach of contract and wrongful dismissal and threatening to sue for compensation. If they had not dismissed him he would not have been in the dock, he said.

As Cochrane's sobbing wife left court she vowed she would stand by him. Cochrane was convicted of providing Sim with the services of Anna Grunt; giving Renfrew a box of cigars containing £50 and a second box with £60; giving Meechan £400, McKay £400, Docherty £250, Silcock £440 and Dixon £3,000. The jury added riders that both Renfrew and McKay sought the money given to them. He was cleared on seven other charges.

Mr Harper asked that Cochrane, who needed psychiatric treatment, should not be sent to jail. After all, the mad, mad world of Cochrane's business had now collapsed.

Sheriff Bell said it was dishonest to offer money to compromise the loyalty of employees of other companies. He accepted the jury's riders but still considered that Cochrane was still culpable, as he had set out to exploit the weakness of others for the benefit of Rotary Tools.

The burly 6ft 4in Cochrane, who weighed 20 stone, was a changed man when he emerged from Barlinnie Prison, Glasgow eight months later. He had lost six stone and was bald and bearded. A chastened 'J.C.' said his farewell party in prison had only run to sweets and chocolates, as he only earned 80p a week. But Cochrane was not quite finished; he regaled newspaper readers for weeks with his revelations of the bribery and sexual high-jinks which had so shocked the strait-laced Scottish business community.

CHAPTER 5
'The Witch'

Politics apart, witchhunts seemed to be things of the past until a young Scots girl, who worked as a nanny for two families in Italy, was branded a witch in 1982 after five mysterious fires broke out in the homes of her employers.

She was dubbed 'La Strega' (The Witch) by the Italian Press after one of the families claimed she had demonic powers and could start fires by psychic means. The British Press took up the cudgels on her behalf as she was kept in an Italian jail for 16 months without trial. One Sunday newspaper even referred to her as 'the British girl trapped by Italian superstition and fear'.

It is difficult now to understand the complex series of misunderstandings which led to Carole Compton, a 20-year-old girl from Ayr, being called a witch. Perhaps it started as a joke over the unexplained fires and talk of the paranormal. In any event, the Cecchini family on the island of Elba are believed to have started it all by alleging she had psychic powers.

The British Press turned up in strength at her trial at Livorno (Leghorn) in December 1983, perhaps intending to show she was the victim of medieval Italian justice. But others interpreted the curious coincidences in her case to mean that she had unconsciously been the focus of paranormal activity.

Carole's Italian adventure, or rather ordeal, began in the summer of 1982 when she fell in love with an Italian waiter, Marco Vitulano, who worked in the Turnberry Hotel in Ayrshire. At that time, she was living with her grandmother in Ayr as her parents were divorced. Carole and Marco became engaged, but Marco had to return to Italy to do his national service and Carole soon followed him to Rome.

Carole did not see much of her fiancé during his military training, even though he was in barracks in the city. His family suggested she could get a job as a nanny and recommended her to the rich Ricci family at the Villa Marguta near the Spanish Steps in Rome.

77

Carole took the job and went with the Ricci family to their holiday home at Ortisei, near Bolzano, in Italy's most northerly province, Alto Adige. She had been there only a fortnight when a large fire, attributed to an electrical short-circuit, partly destroyed the house. They moved to a friend's house nearby but within a couple of days two more fires broke out. One was caused by smouldering paper in a rubbish bin. The other was more serious. At the time it was assumed that all three fires were accidents, and there was no police investigation. Carole was asked to leave because there was no room for her and she returned to Rome. She was then employed by the Cecchini family and taken with them to the grandparents' home at Rio Marina on the island of Elba. In the next two days, several other unexplained incidents occurred. There was a small fire in the room occupied by the grandparents and, the following day, the cot mattress of Carole's three-year-old charge, Agnese, was found burning while the little girl was sleeping in a single bed nearby. Then the Ortisei fires came to light. Carole was arrested on 2 August 1982 and denounced as 'a witch'.

Carole's boyfriend promptly disowned her, and her long ordeal in the labyrinth of the Italian inquisitorial legal system began.

She was to be the victim of the infamous Rocco Code, Mussolini's penal code which became law in 1930 and which, after half a century, still awaits basic reform. Since the Second World War, successive Italian governments have tinkered with the Code but have never been in power long enough to make the sweeping changes required in a modern democracy. Under the Code, people are often kept in prison waiting trial for between three and four years. Such long terms of confinement without trial became more common during the Red Brigade's terrorist outrages.

Had Carole been charged in her native Scotland, her trial would have started within 110 days, as no one is allowed to be kept in custody for a longer period without being brought to trial and must be freed if the rule is not observed. (In England, however, much longer periods of imprisonment are allowed before trial.)

Under the Italian legal system, accusations are made by the police, after which the case is handed over to an examining magistrate who begins the long, laborious process of sifting through the evidence and interrogating the accused and the witnesses before presenting the final indictment for the trial.

Judges in Italy are career civil servants and are not recruited from senior members of the Bar as they are in Britain. Italy also has the equivalent of the Scottish Procurator-Fiscal service, but there the resemblance ends.

No progress was made in the investigation into Carole's case for a month after her arrest, as most of the officials concerned were on holiday. The police did not seize any evidence for forensic examination for several weeks. The little girl's cot, for example, lay outside the house for five weeks before it was collected by the police. The forensic scientist who examined it could find no seat of a fire and assumed the fire had started by 'spontaneous combustion'. This led to allegations by newspapers that Carole had witch-like powers of pyrokinesis — the ability to start fires by psychic means.

After six months of intensive investigation and endless interrogations, the Italian authorities were no nearer to framing charges against the girl, who had spent her 21st birthday in the formidable prison of Livorno, the seaport of Tuscany and the nearest point to the scenes of the alleged crimes on Elba.

Lawrence Nisbet, a well known Scottish advocate who happened to be in Italy about the time Carole was arrested, interrupted his holiday to go to her assistance. Unfortunately, bail for Carole was refused on the ground that no charges had been properly formulated and no trial date set.

Mr Nisbet later withdrew from the case after a disagreement with Carole's mother, Mrs Pamela Compton, who lived in Aberdeen. On his return to Britain, Nisbet said that Carole had all along protested her innocence to the police, the examining magistrates, her own lawyers and everyone connected with the case. She might be a little naive but she had never wavered in declaring she was innocent of any crime, he said. Under the Italian legal system, he added, you almost had to prove your innocence before you were allowed bail.

Although the period of investigation preceding appearance in court is supposed to be *sub judice*, the authorities in Italy kept leaking information to the press.

After two months in jail, Carole passed a psychiatric examination with, in her mother's phrase, 'flying colours'. Mrs Compton said, 'This talk of her starting fires by her mental powers is a load of rubbish, just as I always knew it was.'

But the Italian authorities were adamant that Carole's motive for starting the fires was that the family would then return to Rome, where she could be with her Italian soldier.

This was a highly implausible reason for setting out deliberately to harm a child by setting fire to her cot. In any case, Elba is only a few hours from Rome and Carole was told she could have weekends off. Her letters to Marco from Ortisei and Elba all expressed happiness with her situation and she could have packed her bags and left at any time. The family were, in any event, due to return to their home in Rome within a few weeks.

Moreover, there was nothing in Carole's history to suggest she was so evil as to set out to burn a baby to death for such selfish reasons.

Unlike our adversarial system, in which the defence does not have to be set out until the trial, the inquisitorial system requires that interventions be made on behalf of a suspect at earlier stages. In September 1982, for example, Carole's lawyers were called on to produce expert evidence to refute the theory of her so-called motive. This was difficult to do, given that there is no proper legal aid system in Italy.

Carole's lawyer approached the British Embassy in Milan for aid to obtain a full psychiatric assessment of Carole and of her relationship with Marco but the Foreign Office could not provide such help. Such evidence provided at an early stage could have destroyed the theory once and for all but, in its absence, the allegation of attempted murder was allowed to stand. A fund raised in Scotland to provide bail was used to offset some of her legal expenses. Our legal aid legislation, unfortunately, only provides help for people charged in Britain and not for British people charged under a foreign jurisdiction.

Even one of the magistrates who examined Carole had serious doubts about the charge and pointed out that it lacked a convincing motive for the girl's alleged behaviour. He urged that experts should provide a report, which the defence had been unable to obtain, into Carole's state of mind but a judge refused and the girl remained in jail.

Newspapers in Italy continued to speculate that Carole possessed paranormal powers and that she had the ability to start fires by psychic means. Obviously the authorities were having difficulty finding direct evidence to show she had started the fires or was in a position to start fires at the relevant times and were busy speculating and theorising on possible causes of the mysterious fires.

But the claims of witchcraft and pyrokinesis were dismissed as nonsense by British Consulate officials in Italy and by Carole's lawyer, flamboyant Sergio Minervini, who believed that the rumours of witchcraft had already prolonged the case.

After four months in Livorno Prison, Carole was transferred to Trento, the capital of the Alto Adige region, for further examination and interrogation by another examining magistrate concerning the three fires at Bolzano. Yet a third examining magistrate became involved in the case, causing further delay. All attempts to free her on bail were unsuccessful.

The circumstantial evidence against her was strong indeed — five fires had occurred within three weeks in three separate houses. Her presence was the factor common to all of the incidents.

In April, after eight months of incarceration, Carole was finally charged with three attempted murders and five counts of fire-raising. She was charged with the attempted murder of Mrs Ricci's father, Mario Ricci, and her brother Enrico in the fires at Bolzano, as well as with attempting to murder Agnese Cecchini at Elba. It was grandmother Cecchini who accused Carole of demonic possession and started the whole farcical process in motion.

The next act in the comic opera, which was not a bit funny for poor Carole, came only a month later. The examining magistrate in Bolzano cleared her of two of the attempted murder charges, but given the rights of appeal and counter-appeal by the prosecution and the defence Carole was no nearer freedom. In July the trial date was set for December in Livorno.

Mr Nisbet, who had twice tried unsuccessfully to get Carole

released on bail, wrote to the Foreign Office urging them to bring pressure on the Italian authorities, pointing out that the original argument against granting her bail was that she had not been properly charged and that no trial date had been set. His letter said:

> I am sure you will agree that it is disgraceful that these two simple tasks should take the Italian authorities a whole year to accomplish.
>
> Now that they have been accomplished, is it possible for your department to press for some form of conditional liberty? I know that the examining magistrate, Mr Luigi de Franco, did see a Sister Theresa who runs a girls' hostel in Livorno and agreed that accommodation there, which is available, would be suitable if she was freed.
>
> It is a chilling thought that a wholly innocent person can languish in a foreign jail for a year without trial or any other legal redress.

But Nisbet's pleas were to no avail; Carole remained in custody for a total of 16 months.

On the eve of Carole's trial at Livorno, her Italian advocate, Mr Minervini, called a full-scale Press conference. Unfettered by any law of contempt of court, Italian lawyers, prosecutors and others involved in a case can talk freely to the Press before a word of evidence is heard in court.

Minervini stated he had believed in Carole's innocence since the day he first met her:

'Throughout her three intensive interrogations by examining magistrates both here in Livorno and in Bolzano, she has always denied all the charges and has told the same story — the truth and that is what her defence is based on. She is either an innocent young girl caught up in inexplicable events she does not understand or she is a great actress and mad.

Let's get one thing absolutely clear. This has nothing — I repeat nothing — to do with witches, witchcraft, magic or supernatural powers. The charges are serious enough without all that other nonsense.'

A lot of the evidence against Carole, Minervini said, left great room for doubt. Most of it was circumstantial. The fact that Carole was the only stranger in the households concerned did not make her guilty of attempted murder. There was a lack of hard evidence and Carole herself had always totally rejected any suggestions of the paranormal.

He vigorously thumped his desk as he emphasised that the charges against her were 'truly absurd'. The paranormal theories put forward by the Press might not even be mentioned in court as the prosecution were relying on the motive of the love-struck girl committing 'dastardly' deeds to get back to her boyfriend on the mainland.

Carole had told her mother that grandmother Cecchini never liked her from the start and was very difficult to get on with. Reports in Italy suggested that the grandfather, Mario Cecchini, detested foreigners and that both the grandparents would have preferred an Italian nanny to a Scottish girl who did not speak Italian.

Mrs Compton arrived in Livorno at the weekend to bring Carole a new outfit to wear at her trial. She found her quiet but quite cheerful in the grim Domenicane Prison, only a short distance from the Assize Court where her trial would begin on Monday December 12.

Carole was naturally nervous about the outcome, for a conviction could mean prison sentences of between seven and 14 years. Her mother, however, was quite confident her daughter would be freed. She had not brought any presents for her daughter's birthday on Christmas Eve and said she would get them when they flew home together in a few days' time.

Carole denied all five charges of fire-raising and attempted murder. She was charged with starting the first fire in the Ricci holiday home in Ortisei on 11 July 1982, causing damage of £5,000. She was also accused of starting a second fire two days later in a rubbish bin in the kitchen of the home of Konrad Moroder, a friend of the Ricci's, who allowed the family to move in after the first fire almost gutted their home. She was further accused of starting a second fire in the Moroder house two days later.

She was charged with starting a fire in the bedroom of the grandparents at Elba on August 1, the day after she arrived on the island with Agnese and her mother, Daniella Cecchini. She was accused of setting fire to the mattress in the child's cot the next day while the baby slept nearby in a single bed. The child would normally have been in her cot but her father was not there that week and the child slept in a single bed in the room beside her mother. Because the life of the child was allegedly put in danger, Carole was accused of attempted murder.

There were 14 witnesses cited for the prosecution, conducted by the Public Prosecutor, Arturo Cindolo. Carole had only two witnesses for her defence: her mother and a 22-year-old Lanarkshire girl, Theresa Hunter, who had also been a nanny for the Cecchini's but left suddenly and without explanation a few weeks before Carole was engaged.

Under the Italian system of justice, there were two professional judges, Guido Galligani, the president of the court, and Carlo de Pasquale, who would set the scene and explain the facts at the start of the trial. The judges were accompanied on the same bench by six lay assessors. There were gasps from the British contingent of journalists when all eight emerged from the same door behind the Bench on the opening day of the trial. There was to be no verdict by a jury of Carole's peers alone, as in the British system, but a determination by judges and assessors working together.

The three examining magistrates who prepared the documentary and highly bureaucratic process against Carole played no further part in the case. However, their dubious reasoning and highly debatable findings were to be important factors in the court's deliberations.

For the defence, Mr Minervini handled the charges from Elba. Another eminent advocate, Dr Alberto Valenti, provided Carole's defence for the Bolzano incidents.

Sadly, the case of Carole Compton had by now been turned into a rather squalid battle between lawyers and journalists in the two countries, with the young girl as piggy in the middle. Accusations against her of witchcraft and pyrokinesis had attracted world-wide attention. Many observers felt that the Italian legal system was just as much on trial as the luckless Carole.

The headlines in the Italian Press on the eve of the trial all carried the inference of the supernatural at work: articles entitled 'La Strega', 'Incendaria' and 'Piromane' (Fire-raiser) referred at length to paranormal explanations for the five fires.

There were emotional scenes amid the chaos of the opening of her trial when the world's Press saw the slight girl wanly smiling at a battery of cameras from within a large iron-barred cage built for a terrorist trial five years earlier.

Mrs Compton, outraged to find her daughter in a cage, shouted out, 'She is no criminal.'

Carole, chewing gum and wearing jeans with a new white sweater, kissed her mother through the bars. She also wore a crucifix and a ring that her ex-boyfriend had given her.

Journalists freely interviewed, photographed and filmed her through the bars of the cage. Mother and daughter held hands and Carole announced she was ready to fight for her freedom. She took a tissue from her mother to wipe her eyes as she gazed at the chaos surrounding her. Mrs Compton asked, 'You are not scared, are you? I have waited a long time for this and so have you. Get up there and give them what for.'

For more than half an hour, the courtroom looked more like a three-ring circus than a court of law as more than 70 journalists, television crews, photographers and radio commentators surged forward, climbing over each other and clambering on tables as they tried to get close to the cage. For the next two hours, the scenes alternated between high drama and sheer farce before the trial finally got under way.

When the presiding judge, Mr Galligani, took his seat with the other judge and the six assessors, he pointed angrily at the television cameras and photographers on the high-tiered seating at the side of the court and immediately led the party of officials off the Bench again. The police then cleared the photographers from the court and the judges returned to the Bench.

The names of the 14 prosecution witnesses were called but two were missing. Grandfather Mario Cecchini was ill with a heart condition. The maid to the Ricci family at Ortisei was also absent. Again, the court was adjourned for ten minutes while it was determined whether there were the necessary medical certificates.

As Galligani led his team through the door behind the Bench for the second time, he pointed to a lone cameraman still taking pictures and shouted angrily to the police, 'Why should I have to deal with photographers?' When the court resumed, he ordered the police to give the photographer's name to the clerk of court after his film had been seized. Only then could

Carole's advocate, Mr Minervini make an impassioned plea for her to be released from the grim confines of the cage 'as a gesture to the British Press here today'. He added, 'She is not dangerous and is not likely to escape.'

Galligani immediately ruled she could leave the cage and a chair was provided for her in the well of the court near her lawyers.

Finally, after two hours' delay Mr Galligani said, 'Now we can begin' and the trial proper started. Throughout the first day the 70 correspondents from Scotland, England, France and, remarkably, Argentina strained to hear snatches of Italian and English in the courtroom, a converted convent chapel with a high vaulted ceiling. The second judge, Mr De Pasquale, began the hearing officially by setting out the main facts of the case for the benefit of the six lay assessors who pass for a jury under Italian law.

Carole was then brought to the microphone with a woman interpreter to sit directly in front of the president for a full interrogation on her statements and the statements by the other prosecution witnesses. Again there were constant interruptions as the defence lawyers, time and again, objected to the translations. Mr Minervini asked for a phrase-by-phrase translation of Carole's answers and, at times, it looked as if it was the interpreter who was cross-examining Carole by asking a whole series of questions at once.

The interpreter misinterpreted some of Carole's remarks, taking, for example, 'I was making the tea' to refer to the drink rather than the meal and translating 'short circuit' as 'light bulb'. At one point, Carole, who had been learning Italian in prison from a book given to her by Mr Minervini, dispensed with her interpreter and leaned over to the president's bench to point out something to him in a layout plan.

It was strange to hear no direct evidence given by witnesses, who were merely interrogated by the president based on the statements they had made to examining magistrates — none of which were read out in court. Even the counsel involved in the trial were not allowed to ask direct questions or to cross-examine witnesses but could only direct their questions or objections to the president, who would then ask the witness if he felt so inclined.

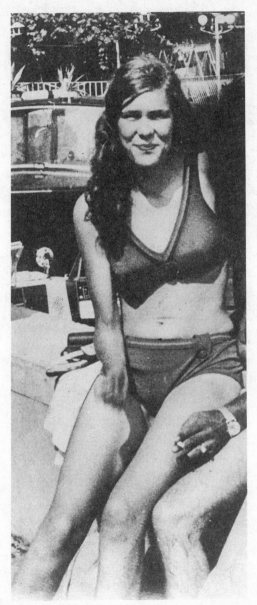

Helga Dumoulin, the 18-year-old German girl, who was pushed from Salisbury Crags to her death by her husband, Ernst, on her wedding day. *Courtesy The Scotsman.*

James Drysdale, the sales director, and Maurice Cochrane, the managing director of Rotary Tools, who faced corruption charges. *Courtesy The Scotsman.*

Miss Anna Grunt, the 25-year-old model who was a principal witness in the corruption trial in which two men were accused of bribing officials in private and state industries with money, gifts and women. *Courtesy The Scotsman.*

Robert Mone, whose ambition was to be as famous as his killer son. He got his way when he was sentenced to life imprisonment for murdering three women in Dundee. Later he himself was killed in prison. *Courtesy The Scotsman.*

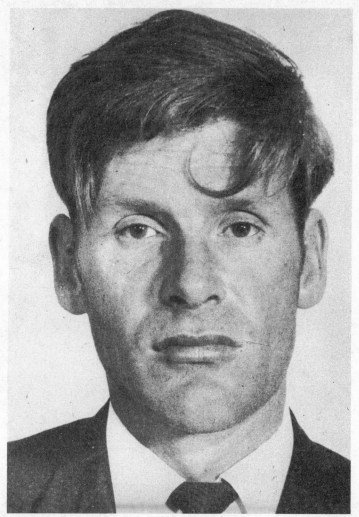

Donald Forbes, who was twice sentenced to life imprisonment for murder, twice escaped, and twice married while in prison. *Courtesy The Scotsman.*

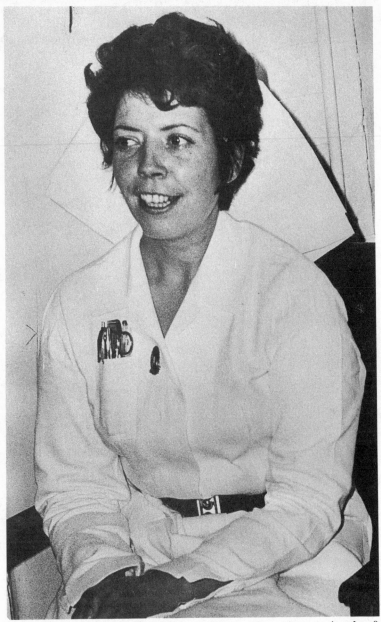

Sister Jessie McTavish in her uniform. She was convicted of murdering a geriatric patient by injecting her with insulin, but was freed on appeal because of a judge's mistake. *Courtesy The Scotsman.*

Sheila Garvie, who was found guilty along with her lover, Brian Tevendale, of murdering her wealthy farmer husband, Maxwell Garvie. *Courtesy The Scotsman.*

Brian Tevendale, Sheila Garvie's lover, being led away by a policeman after being sentenced to life imprisonment for the murder of Maxwell Garvie. *Courtesy The Scotsman.*

Carole continued to strenuously deny all of the charges against her. She made the tea for the little boy at Ortisei and then went outside with the boy to join the maid, Nicole. The only person in the house was the grandfather when Nicole saw smoke coming from a window. Later, Nicole told her everyone thought the fire started because of an electrical fault under the floorboards.

When she was questioned about her statements, Carole said certain aspects were wrong and that she had never made these remarks. They were problems of misinterpretation. Concerning a letter to her boyfriend, she said she was not desperate to get back to Rome because Marco was doing his national service.

During her interrogation she was also asked about mysterious incidents in the house in Elba. A statue had fallen to the ground soon after her arrival, a glass bowl had crashed to the floor without anyone being near it, and a cakestand had fallen from a table. But Carole could give no explanation for such happenings.

A fire chief from Bolzano who had investigated the three fires there said the fact there were three fires involving one family made him suspicious. One of the fires started in a pile of newspapers on a mattress but the flames had travelled downwards which was 'very strange'. There were no signs of any inflammable substances on the bed.

A Jesuit priest from Florence, Father Henry Nolan, who had visited Carole regularly in prison, left the court after the first day carrying a book called, 'Compassion' and said, 'I cannot see how a naive, unsophisticated girl like Carole could commit such an evil deed.'

Even Italian spectators pacing up and down the large open space at the rear of the court felt Carole was innocent and that she should be set free. They pointed to the maxim above the Bench — 'La legge è uguale per tutti' (All are equal under the law) — and said that the charges were 'rubbish'.

As Carole walked into court on the second day of her trial, she was handed two bouquets of carnations by her mother and the former nanny, Theresa Hunter.

Emanuella Ricci, Carole's former employer, said she hired Carole to look after her two-year-old son, Emanuelle. Her son cried every time Carole went near him. When he was only one year old, he was badly burned and every time he touched Carole, he cried, 'She is burning, she is burning.' That meant he didn't like her, as he used the expression to describe any pain or something he did not like.

Signora Ricci was in Paris when she learned of the £5,000 fire at her holiday villa at Ortisei. She could not believe that Carole had anything to do with it but she agreed that Carole did not like being away from her boyfriend in Rome and cried every night. Carole, she said, used to write letters in which she spoke ill of the family. Every time she phoned her boyfriend, she told him she did not like the family and that the little boy did not like her.

Then Mrs Ricci tendered the unthinkable under British law, hearsay evidence, as she told the court what her maid, Rosa, had told her:

> She told me of one occasion when a large picture of Holy Mary fell off a wall then a vase fell down. Rosa said Carole did it and she always told me to give Carole the sack. Rosa didn't like her. The picture was on a wall in a dark corridor. It may have been knocked down accidentally by someone. I did not regard it as a paranormal occurrence.
>
> But any strange episodes, after the picture fell down, were blamed on Carole. When I returned from Paris, Rosa told me the water boiler was making funny noises and that the electric meter had been spinning when Carole was standing near.

Signora Ricci laughed as she added, 'But of course Rosa is a Sicilian and very superstitious. You can speak to her if you like.' However, Mr Galligani, the president, decided it was not necessary to have the direct testimony of the maid to tell of these alleged mysterious occurrences.

The other family maid, Nicole, said she was coming home from the village at about 8p.m. on July 11 and saw smoke coming from a window in the villa. Carole was standing outside with the little boy shouting, 'Fire! Fire!' Although the grandfather was still in the house, Carole hadn't told him.

There was a dramatic confrontation when Carole was brought to the microphone to face Nicole as she gave evidence.

This could only happen under the inquisitorial system, in which the accused are allowed to challenge their accusers directly. Sometimes it leads to the truth but, more often than not, ends in a slanging match.

There was a heated argument between the two girls as to their versions of the timetable of events that day. Nicole's version flatly contradicted Carole's account. Nicole said she went with Carole and the little boy to the nearby village and that she had stayed behind when Carole returned to watch a World Cup match between Italy and Germany on television. Carole told her she was lying and that all three of them returned to the house from the village together.

Professor Pitola Nicola of Pisa University, a fire expert, added further fuel to the controversy when he declared that there was still a mystery about the cause of the two fires on Elba:

'It was very strange that the mattresses burned only on the surface at the same spot although they were made of different types of material. The burn marks could have been caused by a hot iron but not by a cigarette lighter, a match or a naked flame. Both fires had the same characteristics — great heat but no flames. I have never seen anything like it before.'

So much for the prosecution's intention not to dabble in the paranormal!

The Italian Press, too, were in doubt. One newspaper carried the banner headline: 'The Witch-Fireraiser or Simply a Babysitter in Love. Who Knows the real Carole Compton.' *La Nazione* said it was very difficult to understand or explain the mysterious events without going into the difficult world of parapsychology. But the lawyers for the defence had meanwhile ruled out the possibility of calling in an expert on the paranormal.

The Tuscan daily newspaper, *Il Terreno*, carried the headline: 'The Witch Defends Herself. The Scots Babysitter Denies Everything' and *Il Messaggero* in Rome said: 'Free Me. I Am Not a Witch' and 'Diabolical Babysitter — or the Victim of Unfortunate Circumstances'.

The trial descended into pure farce on the third day, when there was a dramatic intervention by a tiny, elderly Italian lady who claimed the Devil, no less, had given her a message about

Casebook of the Bizarre

Carole. Clutching a large wooden crucifix and a bottle of holy water, the woman, dressed all in black, shouted from the public gallery that Carole and her mother were possessed by an eighteenth-century witch but did not realise it.

'I want to touch them and cleanse their spirits', she shouted, and loudly declared her intention to exorcise Carole.

The woman, whose name was Clara Lobina, was well known locally as a faith healer and clairvoyant. She loudly told onlookers: 'When I was asleep last night, the Devil came to me in a dream. He told me to come to court because a witch — she is a young girl — has possessed both the mother and daughter. I have only come to help but I must touch both of them.'

When the court adjourned for a short break she tried to approach Carole, who was sitting in the well of the court between two *carabinieri,* but was led away weeping by two policemen.

Grandfather Mario Cecchini said that when his daughter-in-law, Daniella, pushed open the bedroom door they saw flames coming from the mattress of the cot at the point where it touched the single bed the little girl was lying on. He threw the burning mattress out of the window and the mother picked up the child. His wife saw what had happened and grabbed hold of Carole, who ran away crying and hid in the cellar.

Grandmother Ancilla Cecchini said the only person to blame when the fire broke out was Carole. The flames were half a metre high. She could see the flames from the kitchen. She took Carole by the arms and shook her, saying, 'It was you. It was you.'

She told the court: 'I blamed her because she was the only stranger.'

She said there had never been a short circuit in the house but she agreed the first thing that they did after the fire was to switch off the electricity. She said she smoked cigarettes but denied ever leaving cigarettes burning.

Twice she had said there must be a ghost in the house but when she told police about a statue and a plate falling without explanation, when Carole was not in the room, she did not do so with malice. The police had asked her to tell them everything that happened even if it was strange. She did not really think there was a ghost. It was just one of these things people said when something strange happened. She did not believe in the paranormal either.

But when she was questioned about these incidents, the president told her, 'You are changing your answers.'

Daniella Cecchini, Agnese's mother, told the court that what struck her about Carole was her 'complete indifference'. Carole was a person who moved without making any noise. She told Carole that mysterious things happened only when she was present.

Mrs Cecchini told the court that she had to complain to her mother-in-law now and again about leaving burning cigarettes lying around. Asked whether her mother-in-law was jealous of Carole or the other Scottish nanny, Theresa Hunter, she said she could give the impression that she had no sympathy for British girls. She had a closed personality but there was no ill-will.

Her husband, Luigi Cecchini, said the fire could have been caused by a cigarette end dropped on the carpet. At the time he could not think of any other explanation. Asked why Theresa Hunter left the family, he said she blamed his mother. His mother was against the girl because of her character.

Theresa Hunter said she was never happy in the Cecchini villa on the island and left after 15 days. Her presence was obviously resented. She was treated like a slave and a former au pair left before her because they made her life hell. She added, 'If fires had started while I was there, I think I would have been accused because I was the only stranger in the house.'

Her view was that the fires could have started from short circuits. The electrical wiring in the house was always overloaded.

The two psychiatrists who had examined Carole, Dr Mirella Bertocchini and Professor Ludivico Inghirami, were then brought before the court as a double act to be questioned on their reports. For the first time President Galligani, after being told Carole's personality was 'abnormal', mentioned witchcraft when he asked them: 'Could she have deliberately built this atmosphere of witchcraft for some purpose or, perhaps, for her own amusement?'

Dr Bertocchini at first said she was embarrassed that she could not give a definite answer but after consulting her colleague, she agreed that this type of behaviour could be consistent with the girl's personality. The professor said Carole was responsible for her actions and could not be described as psychotic but an abnormal personality could have 'short circuits' at times of crisis.

She had an abnormal personality but both of them did not want to say whether she would be socially dangerous or not. In certain circumstances, abnormal behaviour could lead to pyromania but Carole could not be described as a pyromaniac unless it could be proved she started any of the fires.

At the start of the final day's evidence, a telegram was delivered to the court from a former employer of the Ricci maid, Nicole. The judges were advised to reject anything she said because she was 'a pathological liar'.

In his closing speech to the jury, Mr Valenti said there was doubt from beginning to end about pyrokinesis. The court was running the risk of convicting a young girl for things for which there was no scientific explanation. They were not just judging Carole Compton but the Public Prosecutor, Mr Cindolo, who was convinced she was guilty.

> How can a young girl described as backward manage to get the exact timing of all these events right? It is not possible unless she is telling the truth.

Mr Minervini opened his speech by saying he wanted to show not just to Italians but to whoever wanted to know, that Italian justice was not 'a farce'. There had been mistakes and misinterpretations all along throughout the trial.

Carole, he said, was the only one who was the stranger and she had been blamed for everything that had gone wrong. The strange things which had happened could not be explained but neither could they be ignored. There was nothing to show that Carole wanted to kill anyone. If she had there were other ways and means to choose which would have made the task easier.

> The normal and the paranormal — what do these things mean? I don't believe in the paranormal but you have to accept that you don't know everything.

Mr Cindolo, in complete contrast, but in keeping with the

more aggressive style of prosecutors under European systems of law, demanded a seven-year sentence for attempted murder and the five charges of fire-raising. The trial, he reiterated, was not about witchcraft. They were there to talk about facts, not fantasies.

> There has been too much talk of objects falling down and of the paranormal and not enough about a child in danger. Just because she has a nice face, an innocent face, it is not enough to sympathise with her. She lied to her boyfriend and the family she worked for. She showed them a face which was not a true face. She has lied in this trial and to the experts and she is cunning.

The trial, he added, was based on an accumulation of circumstantial evidence and allegations. Carole Compton was the common factor in all of the fires. The people in the families were different and the places were far apart but she was there and so were the fires. They could not be explained away as coincidence.

Mr Cindolo said he took responsibility for her arrest but was not responsible for her being in custody for 16 months. This period was necessary because of the special examinations by the psychiatrists and the transfer between the courts at Bolzano and Livorno.

Obviously incensed by newspaper comment in Britain, he concluded: 'This trial is two-fold. There is a trial taking place here and there is a trial taking place in the newspapers. Someone labelled Carole a witch and this has been blamed on the prosecution. This trial is not about witchcraft.'

When Carole was asked if she had anything to say before the court retired to consider its verdict, she replied in a loud, clear voice, 'Everything I have said is the truth.'

The final day of the trial ended as it had begun five days earlier — in utter confusion. The two judges and their six assessors deliberated for six and a half hours before returning to court. Still standing, they delivered their verdict in Italian and hurried out, only to be faced with a battery of television lights and flashlights.

The result of it all was that Carole was freed by a judgment of Solomon.

She was found guilty on two charges of wilful fire-raising at

Ortisei and one charge of attempted fire-raising in the bedroom of Cecchini grandparents at Elba. They held there was insufficient proof on the charges of setting fire to the baby's cot and attempting to murder the child and returned the typical Scottish verdict of not proven. She was absolved on the charge of setting fire to the rubbish bin at Ortisei.

The court passed a sentence of two and a half years but suspended it for five years, thus allowing Carole's immediate release. Carole, laughing and crying at the same time, was quickly led away through a side door to the office of Mr Cindolo to sign her discharge papers. Then she went back to the prison to collect her meagre belongings, five plastic bags and a hold-all, before being driven off for a celebration champagne dinner with her mother.

Carole's nightmare was over. Despite everything, she said she had nothing against the Italian people. All she wanted was to get back to Aberdeen and start her life again.

Back in the court, where the verdict had been read so quickly in Italian that even the Italian Press were confused, it was several minutes before order was restored as journalists argued over translations. Eventually the clerk of court explained the court's judgment and interpreters translated for the British Press.

The incredible, bizarre and baffling trial had a theatrical atmosphere throughout which lent an air of unreality to the whole proceedings. No doubt Carole had a fair trial according to Italian inquisitorial justice but by British standards it left much to be desired. She should have been given immediate translation of everything said in court instead of being accorded this facility only when she was interrogated on the opening day of her trial.

The fact that the case was based on exhaustive statements drawn from interrogations by examining magistrates meant that the president could be selective in what he asked witnesses. Other odd features included the president's decision not to call on the maid Rosa to corroborate hearsay evidence and the assessors habit of mixing with Press and public in cafés nearby during the court recesses.

The length of Carole's detention without trial and the possibility she might seek damages against the Italian state or against the vindictive families who persecuted her was itself a powerful inducement to find her guilty of something. Had she been granted bail on condition she remained in Italy, it seems likely the examining magistrates after a few months of patient inquiries would have decided there was no case to answer.

Amid all the speculation and superstition, one thing is perfectly clear. On the evidence presented, no jury in Britain would have convicted Carole of attempted murder. If her defence had been able to produce expert evidence to destroy the prosecution's ridiculous theory concerning her 'motive', she could well have been released at an early stage in the proceedings. But her prolonged imprisonment and widespread publicity put a few reputations and legal careers on the line. The verdict, therefore, looked more like a political compromise than justice as we understand it.

The British Consul in Florence, Roger Eilbeck, said afterwards: 'I thank God this is over. I am delighted for Carole as it has been a great ordeal for her. She can now go back to resume a normal life. I visited her in prison many times and she always behaved with courage and dignity.'

Almost a year later, an appeal court in Florence upheld the convictions. However, there was a happy ending to the whole saga when Carole married an oil man, Mr Zaroof Ahmed Fazal, who had started writing to her in jail.

CHAPTER 6
The Deadly Mones

If ever there were a reverse case of the sins of the father being visited upon the son, it is the story of the deadly Mones from Dundee, a father and son who between them murdered no fewer than five people over a period of little more than 12 years.

Although the father was no stranger to crime, it was the son who committed the first horrendous murder, that of a school teacher in 1967. The father, who gloried in his son's notoriety, set out to emulate him.

The son is serving the rest of his natural life in prison for murder. The elder Mone, after being sentenced to a minimum life sentence of 15 years for murdering three women, was himself killed in prison by another inmate.

The father, Robert Christopher Mone, known as 'Sonny,' began his criminal career at 16 in 1941 when he was sent to an approved school after committing theft. Later he went to Borstal and then joined the Black Watch, but he was eventually discharged for refusal of duties. When he was 23, Sonny Mone married his pregnant girlfriend, Helen Mullen, against the wishes of her parents. Their son, Robert Francis Mone, was born later in 1947. Young Robert was brought up by his paternal grandparents. The father was divorced in 1958 and married again. He separated from his second wife in 1976.

Robert, like his father quickly established a history of delinquency and escaped from an approved school. He, too, joined a Highland regiment, the Gordon Highlanders, but, as a psychiatrist later told an inquiry, he soon realised he would not get the proverbial field marshal's baton and decided to get out of the army by committing a crime. On leave from Minden in West Germany, he had an argument with his father and bought a gun, intending to kill him. He changed his mind and, instead, committed a crime to 'buy' his way out of the Army. This crime was no ordinary breach of the law.

On the afternoon of 1 November 1967, Robert Mone calmly

walked into a classroom at St John's R.C. Secondary School, in Harefield Road, Dundee, just as a needlework lesson was starting. He was carrying a shotgun.

The police were called after a teacher in a neighbouring classroom became suspicious when she saw that the window of the class was covered over. The building was soon surrounded by officers and firemen. The siege lasted two hours as Mone held the 26-year-old teacher, Nanette Hanson, and her 13 pupils, all aged about 15, hostage at gunpoint. Firemen used ladders in their attempts to reach the classroom. In the meantime, 900 children were shepherded out of the rear entrance and told to go home. After an hour, one girl left the third-floor classroom. A quarter of an hour later, all but one of the young girls ran downstairs crying, suffering from shock.

Then shots were heard. The police, with two priests carrying a stretcher, rushed into the classroom. Mone was cornered by police dogs. Mrs Hanson, from Ilkley in Yorkshire, who had joined the staff two months earlier was found wounded and later died in hospital.

Young Mone, who was 19 at the time, was found insane and unfit to plead when he appeared at the High Court in Dundee on 23 January, 1968. He was charged with presenting a loaded shotgun and sexually assaulting and attempting to rape two 14-year-old girls. He was also accused of murdering Mrs Hanson.

Mr Robert McDonald, QC (now Lord McDonald), for Mone, made a plea that the youth was insane and unfit to instruct his defence. A psychiatrist said he thought Mone was suffering from schizophrenia and was insane at the time of the incident. A second psychiatrist said Mone understood the murder charge but his thought processes were seriously disturbed by schizophrenic psychosis.

Lord Thomson found he was unfit to plead and ordered that he should be detained in the State Hospital at Carstairs without limit of time.

The Advocate Depute, Donald Macaulay, QC (now Lord Macaulay of Bragar) paid tribute to the heroism of Mrs Hanson and a young Dundee nurse, Miss Young, for the way they had acted during the incident. It was quite clear, he said, that the events of that afternoon created a situation of unforeseen and unprecedented difficulty.

Miss Young had been brought in after Mone said he was acquainted with her at one time. Miss Young courageously volunteered to go into the classroom and attempt to talk to Mone. Mrs Hanson, who was in the classroom throughout the incident, took complete control of an extremely difficult situation. She made it clear she was quite capable of handling the situation herself. One false move by people outside the classroom might have led to the death or serious injury of some of the children. As a result of the courageous efforts of Mrs Hanson and Miss Young, the children were ultimately released safely.

For the next eight years, Mone lived at Carstairs. In his room, he had a small library of books on black magic and Nazism. He also had a collection of effigies and a small Buddha in a glass case. After he had been in the hospital a year, he was described by his psychiatrist as 'a potential troublemaker.' Mone complained about homosexual suggestions made to him by another inmate and told doctors that if this was not stopped there would be 'a bloodbath.'

A charge nurse at the hospital said when Mone did not get his own way he could become aggressive but during his stay he did make some achievements. He passed two 'O' and 'A' levels in British Constitution, British Economic History and Law. He failed an Open University degree in law after abandoning his studies but he completed a correspondence course in playwriting and eventually wrote short plays of his own.

He became editor of the hospital magazine. An improvement in his condition was noted until he came under the influence of another inmate, Thomas Neil McCulloch, who was sent to Carstairs suffering from a mental disorder in July 1970 after admitting two charges of attempted murder.

In an assessment of Mone in August 1973, a doctor said, 'He showed a singular lack of appreciation of the feelings of others and was quite incapable of showing remorse or accepting responsibility for his actions.' The doctor added that he exhibited significant characteristics of 'a sadistic psychopath' and that the depth and nature of his offences warranted his continued detention in the hospital because of his 'dangerous and violent propensities.' The doctor's analysis would prove to be prophetic.

About 7 p.m. on 30 November 1976, Mone then 28, and 26-

year-old McCulloch escaped from the hospital in a car, leaving a member of the staff, another inmate and the local village constable dead in their wake. After a dramatic chase involving more than ten police cars, they crashed on the M6 near Carlisle. The general public heaved a sigh of relief when they were taken back into custody.

At first, when they appeared at Lanark Sheriff Court, Mone and McCulloch both denied three charges of murder. Later, McCulloch pleaded guilty to all three murders and to three counts of attempted murder. Mone, however, only admitted murdering the policeman, Constable George Taylor, and attempting to murder three more.

He lodged a special defence, blaming McCulloch for murdering the other inmate, Ian Simpson, and a nursing officer, Neil McLellan. When they both appeared in the High Court in Edinburgh on 28 February 1977, Mone's plea of not guilty to two of the murders was accepted. McCulloch admitted all three killings.

Both admitted murdering Constable Taylor, attempting to murder Constable John Gillies and stealing a police van. They also admitted attempting to murder two workmen, William Lennon and John McAlroy, threatening farmer Rennie Craig of Townfoot Farm, Robertson, and stealing three vehicles.

Lord McCluskey, QC, the Solicitor-General (now a judge), told the court that for several months the two men had assembled weapons, money, a map with a route drawn on it, clothes, a rope ladder, some false papers and a false moustache. Plainly their escape was well planned.

Over the evening of their escape, each of them was collected from his ward and taken to a recreation room for a drama group conducted by Nursing Officer McLellan, who had been at the hospital for 16 years. They took part in the drama group on three evenings a week.

McCulloch was carrying two boxes and Mone a bundle but no one challenged them. Both had been working in the joiner's shop and had made a ladder and a knife. The knife was to replace one from a toolkit in a cupboard of the joiner's shop so that no one would notice it was missing.

Among those who joined the group that evening was patient Ian Simpson, who had taken an Open University degree. A nursing officer, Mary Hamilton, left the group soon after Simpson arrived, as she did not get on with him. The precise details of what happened next are not clear as Nursing Officer McLellan and Simpson were both murdered. It seems, however, that McLellan must have tried to prevent the escape and that McCulloch then savagely attacked him with an axe.

Lord McCluskey told the court that Simpson must have joined in, perhaps to protect McLellan, whereupon he, too, was brutally assaulted and killed. Mone and McCulloch escaped over the perimeter fence. When they were arrested, McCulloch immediately claimed responsibility for using the axe and Mone said McCulloch had 'gone berserk.'

Outside the hospital, they faked an accident. One lay on the road and the other flagged down a motorist, waving a torch. Just as the motorist stopped, a police van arrived and a constable walked towards the two men. The policeman, Constable Taylor, was caught by the throat and attacked by both men using an axe and a knife. The other policeman, Constable John Gillies, managed to radio for help but as he went to his colleague's assistance he got stuck in the boggy ground beside the road.

Mone and McCulloch jumped into the police van and drove off. The fatally injured Constable Taylor was taken by a passing bus to a doctor's surgery. A short time later, ten miles away from the hospital, two workmen, Mr Lennon and Mr McAlroy, stopped their van on the Glasgow-Peebles road to give assistance when they saw a crashed police van, with its blue light flashing, halfway down an embankment. A man in uniform, who had waved them down asked for assistance with a prisoner. But the uniformed man was one of the two accused, and the unsuspecting workmen were suddenly attacked with an axe and a knife. Mr Lennon was repeatedly stabbed in the back. His right lung was deflated and a rib broken with the force of the blow. It was a murderous attack and he could easily have died. Mr McAlroy would also have died if a blow from an axe to his head had landed differently.

McCulloch and Mone drove away in the workmen's van and subsequently, crashed it. They then made their way to a farm. They were bloodstained and wild-looking and still armed with an axe and a knife when they confronted Mr Craig on his doorstep at Taunfoot Farm. They demanded the keys to his car and asked if there were any guns in the house. They ripped out the telephone, which luckily was only an extension, for in the meantime Mr Craig's 12-year-old daughter, realising there was trouble, managed to dial 999. The farmer was soon able to give the police a description of his car. Mone and McCulloch were spotted at Beattock Summit and pursued by police cars over the border into Cumbria on the M6. A police car forced them on to a slip road and they crashed at a roundabout. They then tried to hijack yet another vehicle from someone leaving a pub but were overpowered after a struggle when the police arrived on the scene. McCulloch was still carrying the axe and Mone had the knife.

Mr Donald Macaulay, for McCulloch, said he proposed to say nothing to the court in accordance with the accused's wishes.

Mr Herbert Kerrigan, for Mone, said his client had been progressing well in his studies until he came under McCulloch's influence and stopped his university course. He was persuaded to take part in the escape. Mone wanted to use the minimum of violence during the escape. When he was arrested he did not know McLellan and Simpson were both dead and, in fact, asked how they were.

Lord Dunpark took the unprecedented step of sending Mone and McCulloch to prison for the rest of their natural lives, sentences which could exceed 50 years in view of their youth. Scottish legal history was made when the judge, normally merciful, passed life sentences on both of them and added. 'So far as I am concerned that means life and I shall recommend to the Executive that you are not released until they are satisfied, if ever, that you will cease to be dangerous if allowed to be at large.'

He said these murders were as deliberate, brutal and vicious as any it had ever been his misfortune to meet. This was plainly no ordinary case of mindless murder. They had hatched a plot to escape and were determined to succeed, even if they had to kill to do it.

The curious thing about the disposal of the case was that both men, who had been sent to Carstairs 'without limit of time,' had been examined by psychiatrists after the murders and were found to be responsible for their actions and sane and fit to plead. Yet, eight years earlier, Mone had been found insane and unfit to plead to the murder of the schoolteacher. Such are the vagaries of psychiatric analysis which is often the despair of our judges.

Both men were now said to be 'dangerous psychopaths' with untreatable personality disorders. Another remarkable feature of the horrific story was that both of them were on full parole within the perimeter of the hospital at the time of the break-out.

Afterwards, prison officers and police officers expressed their grave concern at the task facing the authorities of guarding such dangerous psychopaths who had nothing to lose. Mr Edward Taylor, MP, who was then Shadow Secretary of State, called for a special unit to be built for such violent long-term prisoners. Many people were agreed that capital punishment would have been the answer.

The Secretary of State, Mr Bruce Millan, set up an inquiry into the escape to consider the circumstances and the physical arrangements and methods of working and to consider any changes that might be necessary for the safety of staff, public and patients. Sheriff Principal Robert Reid, QC, sitting with three assessors, conducted the inquiry, which began at Lanark on 21 March 1977. The patients' interests were represented by the Mental Welfare Commission.

It was immediately obvious there was an acute conflict between, on the one hand, the nursing staff, represented by the Scottish Prison Officers Association and the Royal College of Nursing, and, on the other, the medical staff.

At an early stage, the inquiry was shown a deadly array of weapons assembled by the two killers, including two garrottes, a number of knives, a hatchet and a 2½-foot sword concealed in a piece of wood.

Detective-Inspector John Fleming of Strathclyde Police told the inquiry that Mone, after his arrest, made a statement in which he said: 'It's too easy to get out of that place. We were supposed to get a day out in Biggar soon but we could not wait. We had been planning this for months.'

Surprisingly, Mone also told the police: 'I have got remorse for what I done. Of course, do you think I am bloody stupid? It was Tommy that done the butchering. He went berserk with the axe.' Mone then started shouting: 'Tommy's a bloody fool. We intended to use the weapons as frighteners only. Nurse McLellan put up a bit of resistance and Tommy lost the head'.

Mone said they had made the knives and 'planked' them in the hospital. They made an impression of a master key concealed in a block of wood in the toolbox. (This was never found despite intensive searches). The two killers had their pictures on false identity cards. Mone had a card bearing the name, 'Thomas Hunt', and the photograph showed him wearing a false moustache and dark glasses. This was how he wanted to appear after his escape.

McCulloch's psychiatrist, Dr Richard Rockstro, was surprised that he had escaped and prejudiced his chances of a legitimate exit from the hospital since he had, in the doctor's opinion, long-term prospects of becoming 'a reasonably safe member of society'.

Unnecessary violence had been used to effect the escape; the doctor agreed that the violence was in fact stimulated by the escape.

Dr John Gotea-Loweg, Mone's consultant psychiatrist, said psychopaths were more of a social problem than a medical one and the place for some of them was not in a hospital. Only time would allow psychopaths to mature. No medical treatment in the form of potions or pills would cure psychopaths, although some did benefit from medical care.

Security at the hospital was strongly criticised in the course of the trial. There had been a general tide of permissiveness in recent years and staff felt they had been neglected by the management committee. General frustration among staff had led to apathy. John Renton, General Secretary of the Scottish Prison Officers' Association, said the hospital management had turned down several staff requests for the appointment of a security officer.

Mr William Horne, who worked at Carstairs from 1948 until 1968 and was principal nursing officer there from 1961, said that Carstairs was the worst-designed top-security establishment in Britain. Whereas similar institutions had connecting corridors allowing patients to be moved at any time of the day or night without being taken outside, the buildings at Carstairs were spread out. Parole within the grounds had been stopped in 1949 after a double murder attempt on the governor's housekeeper and a child, who were both left for dead after a mentally subnormal patient attacked them. Horne said he would never countenance parole within the grounds. There were 34 escapes between 1948 and 1964.

The report by Sheriff Principal Reid, published on 15 November 1977, was thorough and deeply disturbing. It exposed an astonishing catalogue of security weaknesses and recommended nearly 50 precise changes, including a new £1 million inner perimeter fence, floodlighting and a higher level of lighting in the whole hospital complex. Reid called for a major tightening of security, including the appointment of a security officer and an annual inspection by an independent expert on security. He also urged greater control over the work in the woodworking shop, a more careful check on materials used for occupational therapy and the twice-weekly searching of patients. He expressed concern at the apparent ease with which the two inmates had gathered materials to assist them in their escape. Visitors had succeeded in passing to McCulloch a motoring map and a flashlight and Mone had at least £25 which he carried on his person so that it would not be found in searches of his room.

Gifts to patients, Reid recommended, should be placed in closed containers at the gatehouse and opened and searched in the presence of the patient. Patients should be searched occasionally and unexpectedly after visits. The report also called for the installation of devices to warn against attempts to climb the perimeter fence and an effective system to warn local residents of an escape. Sheriff Principal Reid also commented on the lack of communication among the professionals concerned. The psychiatrists of both men were unaware of the extent to which the two patients were contriving to be together.

The report also revealed, from the evidence given outside of the court by Mone and McCulloch, that Nurse Mary Hamilton owed her life to the fact that she had left the drama group when Simpson joined them on that fateful night. McCulloch said he would have killed her if she had remained.

In December 1978, a year after the Mone-McCulloch inquiry, 70-year-old Mrs Jane Simpson was murdered along with two other women in her flat in Kinghorne Road, Dundee.

The other victims were Miss Agnes Waugh (78), who lived in the same block of flats leased to single women, and Mrs Catherine Millar, a 29-year-old bride of only a week who lived at 35 Lansdowne Square, Dundee. Their bodies were discovered when police forced their way into the flat on January 1979.

Miss Waugh's disappearance was reported on 1 January when a district nurse who visited her regularly did not get any reply at her flat. It was later revealed that Mrs Miller's husband, John (40), had called at Mrs Simpsons flat while searching for his bride but got no reply to his knocking. His wife had left home on Friday, December 29 to go shopping and never returned. His wife was particularly fond of old people and enjoyed helping them.

Information from several sources had led her husband to look for her at Mrs Simpson's flat. A short time before he called there a second time, the police found the three women strangled.

On January 18, after two weeks of intensive investigation the police arrested 54-year-old Robert 'Sonny' Mone, who lived at Glenprosen Terrace, Dundee. It was alleged that he had bound the two older women by their wrists and strangled all three, using stockings and an electric flex.

When the trial began in the High Court at Dundee on 25 May 1979, a plea that the charges of murder should be heard separately from other charges was rejected by the trial judge, Lord Robertson. Several charges on one indictment was a matter of everyday practice, he said.

The crucial evidence concerned the events in the Vennel public house in Hilltown, Dundee, on the day of the murders. During an argument with a younger man Mone was overheard to say: 'My son is a murderer. My son will get you. I have nothing to be frightened of when I have got a son.' The barman also heard Mone say: 'My son's a killer.'

Mone was said to have sat, uninvited, at a table with other people and to have kept saying he was 'the Carstairs murderer's father.' The vital witness for the Crown was 21-year-old Stewart Hutton of Sandeman Street, Dundee. He told the court he had met Mone for the first time in the Strath Bar in Dundee that morning. They toured five other public houses and were refused service in one of them. They arrived at the Vennel about 1.50 p.m. and after 2.30 p.m. found themselves alone on the premises with the bar staff. Mone began dancing and singing 'Sonny Mone' and they were asked to leave. They bought beer in a licensed grocer's and made their way to Mrs Simpson's home although Mone at first suggested they should go to the home of his aunt, Miss Waugh, in the same building.

Mrs Simpson and a younger woman, whom he later learned was Catherine Millar, were in the house. The older woman invited them in and all four began drinking beer. Mone suggested they should get more drink and gave Hutton £2 to go and buy a half-bottle. Hutton said he never returned to the flat but, instead, invested the money successfully on dog races in two betting shops.

When he was asked why he did not return to the house with the half-bottle, he said he had felt 'uncomfortable' because Mone had put his hand on the top of his leg and he got the impression he was trying to 'have him on.' Hutton strongly denied the suggestion that he became obstreperous and difficult with Mone and that it was Mone who left the house to get a carry-out, leaving him with the three women.

The court was told that Mrs Simpson had a drink problem, was short-sighted and was weak in her legs. Miss Waugh was not strong on her feet and was not able to get out. She was looked after by a health visitor and a nurse. Post-mortems showed that Mrs Simpson had 204 milligrammes of alcohol in her blood and Mrs Millar 170 milligrammes. There were also traces of alcohol in the blood of Miss Waugh, who was a half-sister of Mone's mother.

The court was told that bloodstains found on Mone's ring could have been the blood of two of the victims. In a statement to the police which was subsequently read at the trial, Mone, referring to his son, said, 'All I live for is to be in there beside him.' Mone had also boasted that he wanted to be a bigger man than his son and often used to tell people, 'I am going to be more famous than the Carstairs killer'.

After a seven-day trial, Mone was convicted by majority verdicts of all three murders and sentenced to life imprisonment. Lord Robertson told Mone: 'You have been convicted of what I can only describe as a terrible crime.

Because of the enormity of the crime, I will recommend to the Secretary of State that you should serve a minimum sentence of 15 years'.

As he was being led to the cells by the police, Monze brazenly shouted, 'Would you mind backdating that?'

'Sonny' Mone's appeal five months later in the Court of Criminal Appeal in Edinburgh was rejected by Lord Wheatley, the Lord Justice Clerk, sitting with Lord Kissen and with Lord Dunpark, who had imposed the whole-of-his-natural-life sentence on young Mone nearly two years earlier.

Lord Wheatley said that he and his colleagues were satisfied there was no material misdirection of the jury by the presiding judge and that the best medical evidence available had been given.

Early in May 1981, young Mone was transferred to the nineteenth-century Perth Prison amid an uproar about security risks. The prison governor, George Dingwall, said at the time that 'more than adequate' arrangements had been made to ensure that Mone remained inside the prison. He assured the public that 'there was no need for anyone to worry.' A Home Office official said that Perth was designed to hold prisoners of the highest security category at all times. Because the prison, flanked by housing estates, did not even have an efficient alarm system to warn local people of an escape, the move prompted calls for new security measures.

The public's fears, as it turned out, were well justified. On May 11 1981 Mone broke away from a working party, leapt on to a rone pipe and shinned up to the roof of the single-storey prison laundry, where he spent the next eight hours shouting about his treatment and claiming that he was locked up for 23 hours a day at weekends. He tore off sections of the asbestos roofing and threw them into the yard and shouted to members of the public only 100 yards away that the prison was 'a powder keg.' Eventually he was talked down by a prison officer and returned quietly to his cell.

The internal inquiry that followed seemed to satisfy the authorities, despite questions in the House of Commons, that security arrangements were adequate. The Scottish Prison Officers' Association, however, expressed their concern at the increasing numbers of mentally disturbed people entering prison.

In the meantime, Mone's father was serving his sentence in Craiginches Prison, Aberdeen. It was there on 13 January 1983 that the next episode of the deadly Mones' story was enacted. In the prison workshop, 'Sonny' Mone was stabbed to death by another prisoner, Anthony Currie, who was serving a sentence for armed robbery.

At his trial in the High Court in Aberdeen in May 1983, Currie denied murdering Mone and lodged a special defence of self-defence. A prison officer said 60 prisoners were having their tea break when he saw Currie running towards Mone. He thought at first it was a high-spirited carry-on but then he noticed Currie had a knife in each hand.

He saw Currie stab Mone in the neck and his left hand move about six times towards Mone, who managed to strike Currie on the head with a tea urn. The officer grabbed Currie, who shouted at Mone: 'At last, you perverted bastard. It's taken me 13 months but I've got you.'

Currie was taken to a cell. As he passed the prison surgery where Mone was lying, he shouted, 'I hope you die, you . . . old bastard.' Later he told a prison officer, 'There was going to be a bloodbath but I didn't have the tools.'

Mone died from two major stab wounds, one penetrating his heart and the other his jugular vein. He had nine stab wounds. Earlier that day he had told other prisoners that he was going to kill Currie. According to one prisoner, Mone said: 'That Cyclops bastard is getting it. I'm going to make him number four.' The other inmate took this to mean that Currie, who had a glass eye, was going to be Mone's fourth murder victim.

Mone had a number of bizarre tattoos on his body, including one on his chest with the initials 'IHS' which, he told another inmate, meant 'In His – meaning the devil's – Service'.

Currie, in his evidence, said he hated Mone, whom he described as 'probably the most obnoxious man in the country'. He had been afraid that Mone and his associates were going to kill him. He said their relationship worsened after he refused to get Mone a jar of glue from the prison cobbler's shop. Mone told him he wanted to give the glue to a new inmate who was a glue sniffer and then commit a sexual act with him.

Mone was furious at not getting the glue and he and his associates carried out a war of nerves against Currie for two months. On the day of the stabbing, Mone came into his cell, held a knife at his throat and said, 'Right, Cyclops, you're off.' He believed Mone wanted to kill him so that he would be sent to the Special Unit at Barlinnie, but he was stopped by another prisoner.

Currie said he had no intention of killing Mone but just wanted to sort the situation out. He described Mone as 'very arrogant and very malignant.' Mone was described by other inmates as a boastful, aggressive person who tried to dominate the prison by bullying weaker, less intelligent prisoners.

At the end of the five-day trial, Currie was convicted by a majority of culpable homicide and sentenced to eight years' imprisonment. He was already serving a seven-year sentence and in 1981 had been given an additional two-year sentence for assaulting a child torturer with a table leg in Peterhead Prison.

Not surprisingly, 'Sonny' Mone's daughter, Rose, step-sister of young Mone, also turned out to have violent impulses. When she was only 16, she was put on probation for three years for attacking a 15-year-old girl, causing her severe injury and permanent disfigurement. A year later, the attacker met her victim again by chance; Rose assaulted her again with a bottle and stabbed her with a knife. This time she was sent to the High Court, where the judge, Lord Wheatley, was less lenient, sending her to a young offenders' institution for three years.

The court was told she came from the notorious Mone family in Dundee, was quick-tempered, had a personality disorder and had received 'a grossly pathological upbringing.' Her father was an exceptionally violent man and there had been gratuitous violence in the home where she was brought up. Rightly or wrongly, she felt the need to stand up for her killer father when she was taunted by people.

Young Mone, now 43, was again in the news in 1988 when he took the Secretary of State, Mr Malcolm Rifkind, to court at Perth for failing to prevent a prison riot. He alleged he had lost a radio, spectacles and other personal possessions when rioters raided his prison cell in October 1987. Mone claimed £120 plus interest and expenses. He accused the Scottish Secretary and the prison staff of fault and negligence and alleged they could have prevented the riot, in which a prison officer was taken hostage and £100,000 damage was caused to the jail's C block.

He claimed that the staff had advance warning that the ringleader, Robert Walker, who was later jailed for a further 12 years, was armed with a knife. No search or other action was undertaken, he said. He was, however, moved to a trouble-free part of the prison. When he returned a fortnight later, he found his cell had been opened and his belongings taken. Mr Rifkind claimed the prison department was not responsible for Mone's loss and that property was held by him at his own risk.

Mone lost his case in April 1989 when Sheriff John Wheatley rejected his claim on the basis that there was insufficient proof that the prison authorities were negligent in failing to prevent the riot. He held, however, that a disclaimer Mone was forced to sign exonerating the authorities for responsibility for his property was not valid.

Mone, slightly-built with prematurely silver hair, appeared in court flanked by prison officers as befitting one of Scotland's most dangerous criminals and gave his evidence from the witness box while manacled to an officer.

CHAPTER 7
Double Time

Donald Ferguson Forbes, known as 'Ginger' because of his reddish fair hair, did not believe in doing anything by halves. A psychopathic killer, he was twice convicted of murder, was twice married while in prison and twice escaped while in custody.

His childhood had been an unhappy one. His father was lost at sea in the Merchant Navy in 1942 and his mother remarried and emigrated to Australia. There was no history of mental illness in the family but young Forbes had mental problems after his father's death. He had no hobbies or interests and became addicted to drink.

On 3 June 1958, Forbes was picked up by the police after a 66-year-old night watchman, Alan Fisher, was bludgeoned to death with an iron bolt in the course of a robbery at the premises of Thomas Devlin and Sons Ltd in Lower Granton Road, Edinburgh. The watchman had been beaten on the head and arms at least 24 times and his skull was smashed into many pieces. Three of his ribs were also broken. A former postman, Mr Fisher was slightly built and was unable to withstand the attack.

A friend of Forbes saw him come into Eddie Carson's Café in Edinburgh about 2.45 a.m. on the day of his arrest. He was very wet and had blood on his trousers and jacket. Forbes told his friend he had been down to Devlin's yard and stolen £10 although, he said his takings should have been about £100. Later in the conversation, Forbes said 'I could be ta'en up for murder tonight.'

Forbes, a 23-year-old fresh-faced, former trawlerman with Devlin's, was desperate for money. The day before the murder, he asked the secretary of Newhaven Trawler Owners' Association for his money from the holiday fund. He was refused, as the money was not due to be paid out until July 1. After his arrest, Forbes sent a letter to the secretary saying that if he had gone to a little trouble over his request he certainly would not be where he was now.

A friend who accompanied Forbes to the Labour Exchange later that day said Forbes had no money and he gave him a shilling for his bus fare. But 'Ginger's' impecunious state did not stop him having a few drinks that night and becoming aggressive and wanting to fight with friends in a bar.

Smartly dressed in a dark blue suit and clutching a white handkerchief, Forbes spoke in a voice which fell to a whisper as he broke down in the witness box in the High Court in Edinburgh. He recalled how he panicked when he was surprised by the watchman. 'I just went berserk,' he told the jury.

When it was put to him that he had made a brutal, savage and sustained attack, involving 24 blows, Forbes replied, 'That's obvious.'

He said he was short of money and out of a job. When he was unsuccessful in getting his holiday pay he went to the unemployment bureau for a job. Describing what happened that night, he said: 'Immediately prior to entering Devlin's I was on my way to Granton Pier where my father's cousin was a pierman. I had a sudden impulse. I jumped over the back wall with the intention of breaking into Devlin's office.'

Forbes told the court that he had the intention of getting the office key while the night watchman was asleep. Instead, he found Mr Fisher standing with his back to him. The watchman turned round and grabbed him by the jacket; Forbes panicked and punched him. Then Fisher picked up the bolt and Forbes thought he might be about to hit him with it,

'I was already in a panic and lost the head. I know I grabbed it out of his hand. I have no recollection whether I hit him or how often I hit him. I just went berserk.'

Forbes didn't think the watchman was seriously hurt, he claimd before the court. He thought someone might have heard the noise of the struggle and he just took the £11.50 from the watchman's wallet and a cigarette case and lighter and left. He was expecting to be arrested on an assault and robbery charge until he saw the papers the next day.

Forbes agreed that drink made him more inclined to lose his temper and get into a panic. He did not think this terrible tragedy would have happened if he had been sober.

Dr Margaret Methven, a consultant psychiatrist at the Royal Hospital for Sick Children in Edinburgh, said Forbes was a psychopath. She had treated him unsuccessfully for more than three years for his mental troubles as a youngster. One of his symptoms was an absence of conscious control. A letter from his mother said he did not appear to be able to behave in a responsible manner for any length of time. It appeared that the search for his father, who was lost at sea, was still going on at the back of the boy's mind. In the treatment centres attended by Forbes at the time, he concentrated on drawing and painting subjects connected with the sea, indicating his obsession with what had happened to his father.

When she saw Forbes in Saughton Prison while he was awaiting trial, Dr Methven formed the opinion that he was rather more disturbed than when she had treated him ten years earlier. Although he could not be certified insane, she agreed he was bordering on madness. There was substantial impairment of his ability to control his actions. His behaviour was not that of a sane person.

Surgeon-Lieutenant Robert Coles told the court he examined Forbes when he was serving on HMS Tyne in 1956. His records from that time described Forbes as 'Below Average – psychopathic type and low IQ.'

At the time of Forbes' trial the penalty for his crime was capital punishment. After a four-day trial, the jury, evidently impressed by Forbes' youth, smart appearance and history of mental illness, made a strong recommendation for mercy. Nevertheless, Lord Wheatley donned the dreaded black cap and sentenced Forbes to be executed at Saughton Prison, Edinburgh on October 16. Forbes, standing between two policemen, listened to the sentence, without a trace of emotion, although three women on the jury wept openly.

A week later, Forbes was married in the prison's death cell to his girlfriend, Rita McLean, an Inverness girl who was expecting his baby. It was the first time in Scotland that permission to marry had been given to a condemned man. Eccentric Glasgow millionaire, the late A. E. Pickard, generously sent £1,000 as a wedding present, obviously feeling sorry for the young couple in their tragic predicament.

Only six days before he was due to be hanged, 'Ginger'

Forbes was reprieved. Edinburgh's senior magistrate, Bailie Herbert Brechin, accompanied by the Town Clerk and the prison governor, read the Secretary of State's message to Forbes, who showed no reaction whatever and made no comment.

Mr John Maclay was one of the last Scottish Secretaries of State to be faced with the agonising task of deciding whether a murderer was to live or die before the death penalty was abolished for good in 1965. He said that after full consideration he felt justified in advising the Queen to commute Forbes' capital sentence to one of imprisonment for life.

In 1969, Forbes was granted parole for varying periods of two to four hours a week and began training for freedom. He was released on licence on 11 May 1970 after serving 11 years and eight months of his life sentence.

Within eight weeks, on 2 July 1970, 'Ginger' Forbes had killed again. The case was most unusual, for he was the first prisoner in 80 years to be released after a life sentence who committed murder for the second time.

Forbes, who was by then 35, had been living for several weeks in the Midlothian hamlet of Newton. On the night of July 2 he was drinking in a public house in Duke Street, Leith. In a brawl outside, he stabbed a man to death and injured his brother. He was then seen walking away with a woman, 'laughing and talking' as they returned to the pub.

Forbes returned to the same High Court where 12 years earlier he had stood trial for the murder of the night watchman. He was now accused of murdering 25-year-old Charlie Gilroy and attempting to murder his younger brother, Robert, who was twenty-one.

The court heard that the two brothers were in the Duke's Head tavern for a darts match when fighting broke out, spilling over into the street. Both brothers were involved and as Robert crossed the road to go back to the pub he was stabbed in the groin by Forbes.

The brothers didn't know Forbes but had seen him in the pub that evening. Robert collapsed at the door of the pub and shouted to his brother, Charles. Later he learned Charles had also been stabbed and they were both taken by ambulance to hospital.

According to one witness Forbes had come out of the pub, drawn a knife and, coming up behind Charles Gilroy, stabbed him three or four times. Forbes then went over to a woman who was standing on the other side of the road. He laughed and talked with her as they went back to the pub.

All the witnesses said the two men were stabbed by Forbes 'for no apparent reason'. Afterwards police found him sitting with two women, calmly finishing his pint in the pub.

Forbes told one of the women he had 'a chiv'. She put it behind a seat but it was later found by the police.

The accused himself was the only witness for the defence. He said that when the fight started there was blood everywhere. He was a bit worried about a friend of his as everyone seemed to be against him. He went outside and found his friend among broken glass. He saw a knife there and picked it up saying, 'There will be no more of that.' He agreed there was a lot of blood on his boots, jeans, shirt and comb case but said a lot of people there got spattered with blood.

He claimed that all the witnesses who had identified him as the man who stabbed the brothers, were 'thugs and villains, the lot of them.' The majority of them were criminals, he said, and were all liars.

In 1958, it had taken the jury an hour and a half to find Forbes guilty of murder by a majority. This time the jury were only out ten minutes before returning a unanimous verdict – guilty: of murder and of attempted murder. On this occasion, there were no tears shed and no recommendations for mercy. However, there was also no black cap, as hanging had been abolished. Lord Stott sentenced Forbes to life imprisonment for the murder and nine years, to run concurrently, for the attempted murder. His refusal to use his powers to order that Forbes should not be released for a minimum number of years created a furore.

Lord Stott said it was very rare indeed for a man released from a life sentence for murder to kill a second time. Forbes' was almost the only Scottish case.

Mr David Brand, QC (now Lord Brand), the Solicitor-General, said drily, 'In the past there were reasons why a person couldn't commit another murder.'

Lord Stott stated: 'Obviously this man will have to be imprisoned for a very long time indeed. Someone else will have to consider some time from now whether he should be released. There will be people better placed than myself who will have to decide what, in the public interest, is the most appropriate date when it does come, many years ahead.'

The statute giving judges power to recommend that in the determination of the minimum time to be served those convicted of more heinous homicides be differentiated from 'ordinary' murderers was ignored by the trial judge. Lord Stott was strongly criticised for his refusal to deal with the question of how long a double murderer should be kept in jail. The public had grave misgivings about the adequacy of the law to protect citizens from such dangerous psychopaths.

The Parole Board who had ordered Forbes' release also came in for a great deal of criticism. They revealed that they had not even seen Forbes before his release and that the reports they had received on him were 'so good' that an interview was not thought necessary. Forbes, they said, had committed the first murder while drunk. However, they noted, once in open prison and once while on a four-hour evening parole, Forbes had become drunk without violent consequences. Unwisely, and with tragic consequences, it was felt Forbes had matured sufficiently to be no danger while drunk.

This misjudgement with respect to Forbes' case made all the more urgent the inquiry set up under the chairmanship of the Court of Session judge, Lord Emslie, to review the law relating to the penalties for murder in the light of the abolition of capital punishment. The committee decided that the life sentence for murder should stand and that it could *mean* life on occasion. There were demands for the Parole Board to conduct their hearings in public following the Forbes case but these were rejected by the Board and the Government.

The Board's reasons for recommending that Forbes should be released left many questions in the public's mind which could never be answered as long as the Board functioned in secret. Nevertheless, the Board's chairman Dr Leonard Small, said that a court of law was precisely what the Board was not. The Board had to endeavour not to retry the prisoner's case. Some of the evidence they heard was of a confidential nature. They were purely an advisory body and the character of the Board would be completely altered if it held public hearings.

An appeal by Forbes of his second conviction was rejected by three judges in the Court of Criminal Appeal in October 1970. He was again smartly dressed, wearing a grey suit, white shirt and tie for his 'outing' from Peterhead Prison.

Forbes told the court: "My conviction was obtained on a prosecution based entirely on perjury. I am not being "a smart Alec" appearing here today. My solicitor was given the names of 12 witnesses who would have testified to my innocence and not one of them was called or even interviewed.

The prosecution was allowed to produce witness after witness. The trial was a farce in this respect – my defence did absolutely nothing I asked them.'

Lord Grant, the Lord Justice Clerk, told him: 'It is clear there was ample evidence from which the jury could convict. It was for them to decide what evidence to accept.'

Less than a year after his appeal failed, Forbes was free again when he made a bold escape from the formidable Peterhead Prison. When the roll call was taken at 6.40 a.m. on 30 August 1971, he was found missing from his cell. Articles lying at the perimeter fence suggested he had gone over the wall. A prison officer found his garage door had been forced and the ignition wires of his car tampered with. Forbes spent two hours in an empty cottage six miles from the prison as a full-scale manhunt was launched in north-east Scotland.

Forbes changed his clothing at the cottage and had a wash and shave. Farmers in the area were warned to keep their shotguns and rifles securely locked up to deny the double murderer access to any weapons. The public were warned not to go near him as he would be desperate and dangerous.

The police were sure he was not being helped on the outside and that, since he was not popular in prison, no one had helped him. Although he had eluded the road blocks, he was still only 13 miles away from the prison. He managed to steal a car from a farm but made his first mistake when he headed for his home town of Edinburgh, for the next day, he was spotted on the outskirts of the city by a policeman in a Panda car. After a chase the police closed in on him when he collided with a parked car in Lower Granton Road, not far from the scene of his first murder. He ran away on foot but his six days of freedom ended with a rugby tackle in a garden. It was a dramatic climax to a 70 mph chase through the busy streets.

Forbes again appeared in the High Court in Edinburgh before Lord Wheatley, who had sentenced him to death 13 years earlier. But, unlike Lord Stott, the judge imposed a four-year sentence for the escape and directed that it should be taken into account, if and when, at any future time, the question of his release was being considered.

Lord Wheatley told Forbes:

> You are no stranger to this court. I have no intention of lecturing you on the nature and gravity of the offences. You are too experienced in serious crime for that to be necessary. In any event, I doubt whether it would have an effect on you.
>
> You took a calculated risk when you committed these offences and possibly you may have thought that, since you are serving a life sentence, you have nothing to lose. If so, I hope to disillusion you.
>
> If a life sentence inevitably meant what it says there would seem to be no point in superimposing another sentence on top of the life sentence but it is common knowledge that a life sentence is reviewed from time to time by the Executive and when this is done, various factors are taken into account.

Forbes had admitted escaping by scaling the prison wall, stealing a car, breaking into an unoccupied cottage and stealing clothing and attempting to steal a prison officer's car from staff quarters at the prison. He walked through an unlocked door after leaving the top security 'A' hall carrying a rope, a broom and a sandbag. He lashed the rope to the brush end of the broom and anchored it over the perimeter wall before climbing over.

Lord Ancram, defending Forbes, said he had always insisted he was innocent of the murder and attempted murder in Edinburgh and believed that certain forensic evidence existed which would prove his innocence. In escaping, he was motivated by a feeling of frustrated innocence. He felt there was no other way to get this evidence.

A few months later, Forbes had another day out from prison when he appealed against the four-year sentence to three judges in the Court of Criminal Appeal. He complained that Lord Wheatley who had sentenced him to death in 1958 was 'a bit prejudiced' against him and that it was unfortunate that he had taken the case.

Four years, he said, was 'an unheard of' sentence for escaping. He argued that Press sensationalism had created so much public wrath that probably Lord Wheatley felt he had to give him a severe sentence.

Lord Grant, the Lord Justice Clerk, said the court was agreed in view of his record and the offences he committed while on the run, that the sentence was justified and in no way excessive.

A Scottish Home and Health departmental inquiry into the escape followed with the usual promises of tightened security but did not prevent Forbes from making another bid for freedom two years later. When he was found missing the police again warned the public that he was dangerous and should not be approached. Road blocks were set up again round Peterhead and tracker dogs were brought in to scour the surrounding countryside.

Forbes had again been found missing when his cell door was opened at 6 a.m. There was an immediate search of the prison. The police searchers were not given weapons at that stage but all reports of stolen vehicles were checked. A full description of Forbes, who was a slim 5'9" with green eyes and reddish fair hair was issued. He had suffered from rickets when he was a boy and the public were told he swung his feet outwards when he walked.

Ten hours later Forbes was found, still inside the prison, in a joiner's shed in the outer yard. He had crossed one of the inner walls but not the outer perimeter fence which had been erected a year earlier following a 27-hour rooftop demonstration. The general public, fortunately, were never at risk but again there was an internal inquiry with more promises to tighten security.

Ronald King Murray, QC (now Lord Murray), who was then Shadow Lord Advocate, called for an objective inquiry and said he would not be satisfied with an internal inquiry this time. He thought it was scandalous that this should happen again and he felt something was radically wrong in the prison. Mr King Murray, had been MP for Leith, when the police car chase two years earlier resulted in the capture of Forbes, his most infamous constituent. Both murders by Forbes had taken place in his constituency.

Forbes' latest escapade coincided with a visit to the prison that day by the Secretary of State, Mr Gordon Campbell, who presented the British Empire Medal to Chief Officer A.G. Campbell in the prison officers' club just outside the perimeter fence.

Patrick Wolrige-Gordon, Conservative MP for East Aberdeenshire, revealed that Forbes somehow managed to cut through the lock of his cell with a hacksaw or similar implement. But how he managed to scale a high inner wall to hide in the shed despite internal searches in the prison was still a mystery. Forbes did not face court proceedings this time and his case was treated as a matter of internal discipline.

But 'Ginger' Forbes had one staunch and loyal friend who was to become his second wife. Alison Grierson, whose stepfather was also in Peterhead, started to write to him. To her surprise, Forbes replied; and they began writing to each other every other day from 1977 onwards. She began visiting him once a month in Peterhead and by May 1978 their friendship had reached the stage where Forbes was transferred to Saughton Prison, Edinburgh for two weeks so that she could visit him.

Forbes' cell was filled with Alison's cards and letters. She had been fostered at the age of two and married at 16. She had a four-year-old son and was divorced in 1979. Forbes was already divorced from his first wife.

Forbes was given permission to marry for the second time – but not in the prison. The prison chaplain made all the arrangements for the ceremony at the local registrar's office on 6 March 1980. Awkward questions were asked in the House of Commons about turning the penal system into 'a marriage bureau'. The proposed ceremony followed the wedding of killer Jimmy Boyle, an inmate of Barlinnie's special unit two months earlier and MPs were naturally anxious that the authorities should not be seen to be giving special treatment to killers.

A crowd of 300 gathered outside the registrar's as Forbes arrived, accompanied by two prison officers in plain clothes. He was not handcuffed. Two detectives followed in another car. Alison, who was then 24, had arrived a few minutes earlier in a car driven by the best man, Jim Brockett, the port

missionary for the British Sailors' Society. Her wedding dress
and ring were bought from the money Forbes received after
some his clothing was burned in a fire during the rooftop
disturbances at the jail a year earlier. The ring had the
inscription: 'D–A=O. (Donald Minus Alison Equals Nothing.)
Forbes presented her with a single rose at the ceremony.

When the happy couple emerged they stood on the steps for
a few minutes kissing and hugging. The new Mrs Forbes said,
'I am absolutely delighted, I love him so much.'

Forbes, too, said he was very happy as they left for the
prison, where they were allowed 90 minutes together. Later in
the day, they had another visit and shared a wedding cake
given anonymously by someone in Peterhead. Afterwards,
Alison said: 'I thought the whole day was very nice. I couldn't
have wished for anything better. Everyone has been very kind
to us today.'

She realised there would be a lot of interest in their wedding
but was surprised at the size of the crowd. She heard some
shouts of 'Bring back hanging' but they were drowned out by
the cheering.

She remarked: 'A lot of people have said "You are daft." But
it is going to make a great emotional difference to me. Nothing
can ever hurt me while I am with him. I certainly don't think of
Donny as a double murderer. It is not that I disregard what he
has done. I know only too well.'

When Alison, accompanied by her son and Mr Brockett,
went back to the guest house in Peterhead where she had been
staying, they were at first refused entry because of all the fuss.
Eventually, after some persuasion by Mr Brockett, they were
allowed to stay.

Five months later came another shock when Alison
announced she was expecting a baby and that the conception
had taken place in Peterhead Prison just after the marriage
ceremony when they were left alone. The baby was due on
November 30 but arrived prematurely in October. One of the
nursing staff at Aberdeen Maternity Hospital phoned the
prison so that Forbes could be given the happy news. The baby
was named James after Forbes' best man, Mr Brockett.

Prison officials strongly denied that Mrs Forbes became
pregnant behind bars. A Scottish Office official said the

prisoner was escorted throughout the whole ceremony and afterwards until he returned to his cell.

Mrs Forbes began living in a caravan near Peterhead with her two children. She applied for a local council house but was refused by local councillors because she had no connections with the town. In the meantime, Forbes had asked for home leave and conjugal visits by his wife, these requests were also refused.

The strain of it all took its toll on Alison and in 1986 she filed for divorce at Aberdeen Sheriff Court. She claimed the marriage had broken down irretrievably because they had not lived together for five years. But Sheriff Andrew Murphy refused to grant her a decree and raised the question of whether she knew when she married him that there was little chance of them living together. He remitted the case to the Court of Session in Edinburgh because of the unusual circumstances; indeed, there was no precedent. The case was later dropped.

Forbes is now in his 31st year as a prisoner. He will continue to be Scotland's longest serving 'lifer' for a long time to come and it will be a brave Parole Board that sanctions his release into society on parole for the second time.

CHAPTER 8
The Untraceable Poison?

In fiction, the hormone insulin, although the lifeline for diabetics, has always been represented as the perfect murder weapon because it could not be traced. But in a case in 1974, scientists and the world authority on insulin, the Wellcome Foundation, proved that abnormal quantities of the hormone could be shown to be present in human tissue provided samples were taken within 16 hours of death.

Poison has always been the favourite weapon of women murderers. Out of 68 women hanged for murder in the UK over the last century, 37 of them were poisoners. Arsenic, strychnine and phosphorus, all used in rat poison, were for many women easiest to obtain.

But for women in nursing, the choice of poison was always wider. The most infamous nurse of all was Catherine Wilson who, in 1863, became the last woman to be hanged in public in London. Her weapon was colchicum, which like insulin, could not be traced in the bodies of victims. Then there was Nurse Waddingham, hanged in 1936 for murdering two elderly patients in her Nottingham nursing home for their money, using morphia.

The complex trial of Sister Jessie McTavish, like that of the infamous Madeleine Smith, became a *cause célèbre*. Euthanasia was suggested as the only possible motive for McTavish's murder of a geriatric patient in her ward at Ruchill Hospital, Glasgow by repeatedly injecting her with insulin. McTavish was convicted of murder and sentenced to imprisonment for life but, on appeal, was freed because of a judge's mistake in charging the jury.

There were wild rumours in June 1973 concerning Ward 5 at Ruchill following a spate of sudden and unexplained deaths. The suspicions of an auxiliary nurse, Rose Hazlitt, were aroused when the third death occurred. She spotted a bruise on the patient's arm which could have been caused by an injection and found that none had been authorised by a doctor.

After the sister went off duty, she searched the ward and found three empty insulin containers and used syringes in a bin. She raised the matter with another sister who told her she was making a very grave accusation. Nonetheless, the wheels had begun to turn. The police were called to the hospital on 2 July when a doctor refused to sign a death certificate.

When Detective Inspector Sinclair Paterson walked into the hospital on that day he thought he had a simple inquiry on his hands. Instead, he found himself faced with the most difficult and baffling investigation in 28 years of police work. Known to the underworld as 'Daddy Fox', he set up his headquarters in a small room at the hospital and remained there for two months. He rapidly became an expert on drugs, poison registers, hospital procedures and intricate scientific and medical data. No one came forward with information and, as one weary detective put it at the time, 'Breaking down the closed shop of the medical profession was like drawing blood from a stone.'

The scientists found that insulin disappears from the body within 12 to 24 hours of injection and only at the point of entry do traces remain longer. The Wellcome Foundation at Dartford, Kent carried out the vital tests but inquiries spanned the world as witnesses were contacted in New Delhi, Khartoum, Nigeria and several cities in the United States.

Of the five recent deaths in the ward, the one that concerned the police was that of 80-year-old Mrs Elizabeth Lyon. The case became the most complicated medical and scientific investigation handled by the police for many years. They decided to charge Sister McTavish but were in a quandary as to what the precise charge should be. Finally they settled for an assault charge as the safest option. McTavish remained in custody for 87 days until she was released on the order of three High Court judges because the Crown could not bring her to trial within 110 days – the period stipulated in Scots law as the maximum for an untried prisoner to be kept in custody. She was later charged with murder and assault but remained free, thus becoming the first person ever to remain at liberty, awaiting trial, on a charge of murder.

When dark-haired, attractive, 34-year-old Jessie McTavish known as 'Jay', a dedicated nurse with a merry laugh, was called to the Nursing Superintendent's room in June 1973 she thought she was being promoted.

'Instead I was suspended and asked about an ampoule of insulin. I was just so bewildered. Nobody could tell me what was happening, I couldn't even cry,' she said afterwards.

She also said:

> I just could not believe what was happening to me – being accused of assaulting three old pets by injecting them with something not medically prescribed. My mind went blank. Later I knew the authorities suspected me of euthanasia but they were so wrong. That was rubbish. My instinct and training was to save life, not to destroy it.
>
> I have a special feeling for old people. They are in the twilight of their lives and there is nothing more tragic than to watch the humiliation of old people. So many of them go into geriatric wards and are there until they die. Once they are in, few families want to take the responsibility of looking after them. This is the real humiliation of old age. It robs them of dignity and they cannot hide the hurt and neglect.

All along, she emphatically denied committing euthanasia and when her trial began in the High Court in Edinburgh on 17 September 1974 pleaded not guilty to all charges.

She was accused of murdering Elizabeth Lyon by repeatedly injecting her on 30 June 1973 with soluble insulin which was not a necessity of her treatment and was without medical authority or prescription, in consequence of which Mrs Lyon died next day.

She was also accused of assaulting four other elderly women patients by giving them unauthorised injections, three of them soluble insulin and the other, pethidine. Two of the patients, it was disclosed, had since died. Two further charges of forging a doctor's signature on the ward's dangerous drugs register were dropped at the start of the trial.

As the trial developed, the revelations of what went on in a geriatric ward in a large city hospital shocked the public. Large queues formed outside the High Court in Parliament Square each morning as spectators made sure of a seat in the restricted public benches of the same court were, more than 100 years earlier, Madeleine Smith had been accused of poisoning her lover.

The case unfolded as the jury heard how Sister McTavish's moods would swing from euphoria to deep depression within minutes, about strange episodes in which she had been involved and about her sometimes bizarre behaviour while on duty.

Among the first witnesses was an auxiliary nurse, Jean Clark, who recalled that Sister McTavish had once told her and another nurse in the dining room about an episode of *A Man Called Ironside* in which no trace of an injection could be found in the body of a murder victim. Sister McTavish, she said, gave no indication of what substance she was referring to. Clark also said that on Sunday, 4 June 1973, the day before one of the patients, 71-year-old Martha Devine, died, she saw Sister McTavish give her an injection of pethidine. Later, she saw her drawing up a syringe and going behind the curtains at Mrs Devine's bed. Sister McTavish was in her stockinged feet. She told Clark 'She's only got five minutes.' Clark was shocked by the remark. 'It was very unusual for her to say something like that. She always fought for a patient's life. I felt like hitting her for the way she was acting.'

Charles Carr, a charge nurse at Stobhill Hospital, Glasgow who trained with Sister McTavish, visited her that evening in the ward. He must have looked surprised at the rather large dose of pethidine – something like 400 milligrammes – which he saw her preparing for Mrs Devine. McTavish simply said, 'Doctor likes patients to go quietly.'

But the patient's daughter, Maureen Devine, told the court that Sister McTavish's attitude towards her mother had always been one of kindness. She knew her mother was dying because her condition was rapidly worsening; semi-conscious, she managed to say, 'Goodbye'. Miss Devine was very upset and Sister McTavish stayed with her overnight.

'I was grateful to her for her help and her company that night,' she said.

She saw Sister McTavish give her mother, who was still unconscious, two injections of pethidine and then a third injection sometime later. It was obvious to anyone, even a non-medical person, Miss Devine told the court, that her mother was dying. Later she was told her mother had died. Sister McTavish again spent the night with her and also attended the requiem mass and the funeral.

Asked about her mother's care in the hospital, she said, 'Mother would not have lived so long, had she not been so well looked after.'

An auxiliary nurse in the ward said that in the last few days of June, Sister McTavish did not seem to be as caring as usual. When the police arrived after the deaths of three geriatric patients in a week, McTavish said, 'Do they want them to live forever?' Asked if anything was said about tracing an injection, the auxiliary testified that McTavish told her, 'Even if I did it, they would never trace it.'

She saw Sister McTavish inject Mrs Devine in the thigh on June 24. She had never seen an apparently unconscious patient being injected before. She asked the sister why she was giving the injections. McTavish explained it was vitamins. The sister asked her to go to another ward for insulin. She brought back a carton and shortly afterwards saw McTavish filling a syringe. Later she saw a small puncture and bruising on Mrs Lyon's arm. She told the sister she had seen her injecting the patient.

A domestic help testified that she saw Sister McTavish injecting Mrs Lyon. Asked if there was anything different about the sister, she said: 'I don't know. She just looked different. Her eyes looked glazed. She did not look herself.' Normally the sister was quite a jolly person but, at the time, there seemed to be something unusual about her. When she came to work the next day, McTavish told her that Mrs Lyon would 'go that morning.'

A student nurse said the staff were upset the next day when Mrs Lyon died. She asked the sister what had happened. She replied, 'Mrs Lyon hd a cerebral last night.' Finding the student and another nurse in tears in the locker room, McTavish asked what was wrong; they did not answer. Then McTavish said, 'No one saw me give an injection.' When the other nurse said she did, the sister said, 'No. I was taking off blood.'

Mrs Janet McLean, who was a student nurse in the ward, said that on Monday, July 2 she learned that police were making inquiries. She was sitting with Sister McTavish in the dining room; the sister said they had been questioning her about insulin and that she had told them, 'I didn't do anything,' and that they couldn't trace it anyway. 'She said she told them up at staff administration that they could dig up the bodies if they liked but they would not find any trace of insulin, even if she had given it, which she had not.'

Later that evening, Sister McTavish was suspended. Mrs McLean described McTavish's strange attitude during the few days before: 'We did not know what she was going to say or do. She walked about in her stockinged feet and had a bath in the ward, which was unhygienic. Her eyes were glazed most of the time.'

Mrs McLean saw the sister give three injections on June 24. When she asked why one patient was getting pethidine, McTavish replied that the patient was choking. McLean, however did not see her choking. The sister told her she could give the next injection and showed her where to inject Mrs Devine with pethidine. She wondered why pethidine was being used as it was not indicated on the patient's treatment card and there was no record that she had been given the drug.

The next witness, Night Sister Aileen Bryce, raised the issue of the difficulty of getting doctors to come to the geriatric ward and the problem of their 'moonlighting' in private practice, which was to lead to a full inquiry by Greater Glasgow Health Board and a general tightening-up of procedures.

Sister Bryce said that Dr Ram Saxena and his wife, Dr Usha Saxena, were responsible for the patients in the ward. On June 30, when Mrs Lyon was semi-conscious, Bryce telephoned Mrs Saxena. 'She asked me what I thought she could do for the patient.'

Asked by Mr Donald Robertson, QC, for the defence, if that was an odd thing for a doctor to ask, Sister Bryce said, 'I would have thought so.' When the doctor came to the ward she merely asked Mrs Lyon if she wanted the window open; then she turned and walked out. Sister Bryce did not see the point in asking a semi-conscious patient if she wanted the window open.

Asked if she had any difficulty contacting the Saxenas, Bryce said she remembered calling Dr Ram Saxena one evening but he did not even come to the ward. He instructed on the telephone to administer a pain-killing drug to a patient, telling her what drug and the dosage. When a doctor prescribed a drug by telephone, Bryce explained to the court, he had to sign the ward record within 24 hours. But on one occasion she remembered, Dr Saxena did not do so.

Sister Bryce said they had most difficulty getting in touch with Dr Usha Saxena to come and see patients. There were also occasions when Dr Ram Saxena and another doctor were supposed to be on duty in the hospital yet calls were put through to their homes.

Asked if she had difficulty in getting doctors to look at the body when a patient died, Bryce said that doctors signed death certificates without examination on numerous occasions.

Dr Ram Saxena told the court he had not prescribed injections for any of the five patients named in the indictment. Neither had he prescribed injections by telephone. He had not authorised pethidine for Mrs Devine.

However, he admitted making two mistakes in the cremation certificate for Mrs Lyon, saying he had seen her four hours before her death when, in fact, he had seen her 19 hours before. He also said he had seen the body ten hours after death but in fact had viewed it 24 hours later. 'I must have been in a hurry when I put down these times,' he told the court.

Under cross-examination, the doctor admitted he had not told his consultant or another superior that he was doing outside work as a locum for general practitioners during this period:

> After 1pm I am free and no one can do anything about it apart from the income tax man. Apart from one or two exceptions, everyone is doing this. Everyone works but no one tells. I really want to make a career by working hard. I was trying to impress doctors that I can work as a GP so that I can work in future, if I want to, as a GP.

He denied having an arrangement with a hospital telephonist regarding how to handle the situation if he could not be reached because he was outside the hospital.

A 60-year-old former sister, Mrs Sybil Wishart, who had worked in Ward 5 with the accused, told the court she had reported Sister McTavish's behaviour several times but nothing had been done about it. She thought that McTavish needed help and denied there was 'bad blood' between them. She agreed she wrote letters to Maureen Devine, the daughter of the patient who died, telling her she had resigned after being accused of slander and telling lies. She also said in one letter she had reported Sister McTavish several times.

Mr Robertson, 'You had made up your mind she was guilty?'.

Mrs Wishart replied, 'I had not made up my mind. No one is guilty until they are proved guilty.'

Just before she was arrested on July 2, Sister McTavish told her, 'They are making a fuss about the death of an old woman.'

Mrs Wishart said she told the other nurses, who were crying, that Sister McTavish had been taken away. She told them to buck up and that if they saw anything unusual to come and tell her. Later an auxiliary nurse brought her a disposal bag containing several bloodstained syringes and a love letter, written to James McDonald, a charge nurse who worked in Ward 21.

The passionate letter, written with schoolgirl fervour, was read in court:

> Dear James. Have I told you how much I love you. To be alone with you is to be walking through heaven. For the stars hold me in their magic and their light is competition in my eyes. I love the way you look at me and physical contact is so necessary. Oh, my darling, can't you see I am so deeply in love with you. My whole being cries out for you and I adore you. I only wish you could adore me. Ever loving, Jay.

James McDonald told the court that he had never received the letter. He had, however, been pestered by Sister McTavish. She was very demanding. They met as students and he had taken her out on social occasions but her passion was unreturned.

A sister in charge of another ward told the court that on July 2 Sister McTavish came rushing into her ward saying she had an emergency on her hands and required some insulin. When she gave her a bottle McTavish erased the ward number and put down Ward 5. When the charge nurse asked what she was doing, McTavish replied: 'Sister Wishart will get me into trouble. She has reported me for borrowing insulin.'

Dr Chamand Annand told the court it was normal practice at Ruchill for doctors to sign death certificates even when they had not attended the patient during their last illness. He added, 'You don't have to know every patient who dies but you do have to certify death.'

When Dr Annand was asked if he was aware that this practice was not strictly in accordance with the law, Mr John H. McCluskey, QC, the Solicitor-General, (later to become a Life Peer and a High Court judge) objected, saying he did not see what this had to do with the case.

Mr Robertson, for the defence, said:

> There has been a great deal of evidence that Sister McTavish has not obeyed hospital procedure and has done things not strictly according to the rules. It has been suggested there is something sinister in these breaches. But it is highly relevant to inform this court to show that departures from procedure were common in this hospital and that there is nothing sinister or significant in deviations that may have been shown.

Lord Robertson said, 'I won't stop you but the witness said it was common practice in all hospitals.'

Mr Robertson then said to Dr Annand: 'I am not trying to trap you but you were aware that the way you signed death certificates in relation to Mrs Lyon and Mrs Devine was not proper? Dr Annand replied: 'I didn't say that. This was the accepted way. We have done it always.'

Re-examined, the doctor agreed it was very desirable that a certificate should be issued as soon as possible after death, in order to avoid the body lying in the ward with other patients until the doctor who had been attending the patient was available. He had signed death certificates on Mrs Lyon and Mrs Devine after making external examinations and seeing the medical records and on information given by the ward sister. He was not given any information about the patients receiving injections.

If he had known Mrs Devine had received six injections, Dr Annand stated, he would not have certified the death. Nor would he have signed a certificate for Mrs Lyon if he had been told she was not given normal injection treatment.

A research biochemist from the Wellcome Foundation told the court there was clear evidence of needle tracks on tissue samples from the body of Mrs Lyon. Tests showed activity in forearm tissues which could be attributed to insulin. A blood sample, however, proved unsatisfactory for the detection of insulin.

The man who led the investigation, Detective-Inspector Paterson, said that when he arrived at the hospital on 2 July he met Sister McTavish, who told him the doctor who had refused to sign the death certificate was not in the ward.

She then said: 'Are you going to put the handcuffs on me? If you are so minded, it is a pity because I was going to do a spot of fishing.' She told him senior nursing staff had been looking for insulin. She then gave him a yellow carton from a cupboard, saying 'Here is insulin.'

It was the first time he heard the word 'insulin' in the course of the inquiry. After he learned of allegations of unauthorised and unrecorded injections, he thought it imperative that Sister McTavish be suspended from duty. She agreed to go with him to the police station but she was not arrested at that stage.

When the Detective-Inspector cautioned her, she replied, 'Now you promised me a well done steak.' She declined the services of a solicitor. Paterson charged her with assaulting Mrs Lyon and two other patients by administering an unknown substance. There were gasps from the public benches as Inspector Paterson reported Sister McTavish's replies to the charges.

When he charged her with assaulting three of her patients by administering an unknown substance, she said, 'I gave ½cc of insulin soluble to Mrs Lyon only because she wanted to be put out of pain and misery.'

When the charges were again preferred at the bar of the police station, Sister McTavish said: 'I gave Mrs Lyon a ½cc of soluble insulin. She was taking a cerebral and was wanting out of her misery.'

Jessie McTavish's alleged replies went a long way to convicting her of murder, although she denied throughout her trial that she ever made such confessions. The judge's failure to remind the jury of this vital fact brought her eventual release on appeal.

The Chief Nursing Officer at the hospital, Alfred Portwin, who was present when Jessie McTavish was cautioned by the police concerning allegations of illegal injections, said that before being taken to the police station, she said 'I hope I get steak and chips for my supper.' Asked if this was a flippant reply, he said, 'My feeling was that Miss McTavish failed to understand the seriousness of the situation.'

Miss Jane Hastie, Principal Nursing Officer of Glasgow Northern Group of Hospitals, agreed that there never could be an occasion when a nurse could administer a drug not prescribed by a doctor. She could not envisage a junior doctor giving a nurse instructions to give whatever treatment she liked to patients.

The prosecution case against Jessie McTavish was building up slowly but surely as doctors, nurses and experts in the medical profession condemned her practices in Ward 5. Dr Thomas Judge, a consultant at the hospital, said he was staggered when he learned of patients in the geriatric ward receiving injections and he thought the ward sister had 'lost her reason.'

He was very worried after examining the body of Mrs Lyon. He then went to see the patients in Ward 5 who had complained about receiving injections. Mrs Agnes Rowan, who was 67, told him she had been given an injection by Sister McTavish and said it had made her feel ill. She said she had sweated and felt cold and hungry. He recollected that she also said she thought she was going to die. Mrs Mary Logan, also 67, told him she, too, had received an injection. "Then she stopped speaking and looked very frightened', Dr Judge told the court. When he asked her who had given the injection, she said, 'A nurse.' Then Sister McTavish, who was present, said under her breath, 'Sterile water. Sterile water.'

He then examined the forearms of every patient but felt that a full head-to-foot examination would only make worse the already demoralised situation in the ward. He was already staggered about the injections and he said he was going to notify the Procurator-Fiscal. He thought the sister had 'lost her reason'. Sterile water was not used, as far as he knew, as a placebo in Ruchill. The only time it might be given, Dr Judge stated, was orally in place of a sedative.

Professor Gilbert Forbes, Regius Professor of Forensic Medicine at Glasgow University, who carried out the post-mortem on Mrs Lyon, said there was evidence of a cerebral haemorrhage in 1969 but nothing to show she had suffered one more recently than that.

She was not a diabetic and his examination failed to reveal why she should have died in the way and at the time she did. He agreed with the opinion of Professor John Owen that Mrs Lyon received an injection of at least 200 units of insulin 14 hours before her death. He accepted that the cause of death was insulin poisoning.

The Crown case had ended with a damning catalogue of malpractice. Jessie McTavish had a lot of clear evidence to refute when she took the witness box for two days.

Speaking in a clear voice that was sometimes tinged with emotion, she strongly denied ever giving any of her patients insulin injections. When she was summoned before the Chief Nursing Officer she thought she was to be promoted:

> He asked me if I had any idea why I was being sent for. I said I thought it was for promotion because I had been on a course for the care of the elderly. He said he was sorry it wasn't that. It was about injections.

She agreed before the court that she had injected pethidine by agreement with a doctor and had given other medication by injection. She had also given other patients injections of sterile water as a placebo. On June 24, when Mrs Devine was very ill and not expected to live, she spoke to Dr Ram Saxena in another ward. He told her: 'You are trained. Give her what you like.' She said, 'What about pethidine?' and he agreed. 'We discussed elderly patients. His views were that these patients were old and dying anyway, which annoyed me.'

She gave pethidine to Mrs Devine and also injected Lasix and later Largactil, as the patient could not take her normal oral dose. She agreed that when a male nurse visited her that evening she told him, 'Doctor likes them to go quietly.' This was not an abnormal remark to make in a geriatric ward.

She denied giving another patient, Mrs Margaret Ward, an insulin injection. She gave her an injection of aminophylline as she felt it would act more quickly. She agreed she sent a nurse for soluble insulin as she was expecting two diabetic patients from Stobhill Hospital.

Mrs Ward died that night. Sister McTavish agreed she told a

relative in the mortuary, 'They call me Burke and Hare.'

Asked if this was just a joke in bad taste, she replied, 'Yes, but if you saw our mortician you would probably appreciate the joke.'

She attended the funeral of Mrs Devine at her daughter's request on June 27. On June 30, she noticed there was no insulin in the ward and thought it very odd. They had obtained insulin from the pharmacy four days earlier. That day she gave Mrs Lyon pethidine and later an injection of sterile water. Mrs Lyon was drowsy and lethargic and complaining of pain. She tried to contact Dr Ram Saxena first but he was nowhere to be found in the hospital. His wife, Dr Usha Saxena, also did not answer the call. McTavish left instructions with the switchboard to ask Dr Ram Saxena to come to the ward.

In the meantime, she thought she would try out the patient with a placebo. The use of sterile water as a placebo was 'not uncommon', Sister McTavish testified. It seemed to calm down Mrs Lyon and two other patients wondered why they had not been given an injection or seen the doctor. She gave them each an injection of sterile water.

She borrowed two bottles of insulin from other wards that day. When she came on duty on July 1, she learned Mrs Lyon had spent a very poor night. There was a bruise on her right arm and a puncture mark and there was a query in the report as to whether blood had been taken off.

She noticed some syringes lying about and assumed the doctor had been to the ward. Mrs Lyon died at 11 a.m. McTavish presumed, she told the court, that the patient had suffered another cerebral haemorrhage.

When she was asked about her relationship with Sister Wishart, McTavish said it would be more than fair to say there was no love lost between them. On two occasions Sister Wishart had got her into trouble.

She agreed that when the two policemen arrived, she had talked with them about prison life and food. She asked them if it was a fallacy about bread and water and the inspector said something about a well-done steak. She told them if she got into bother she hoped that was what she would get.

She returned to the ward to find it in 'utter chaos'. 'All my staff were hysterical, crying and upset. I made a cup of tea and told them to pull themselves together. I said the gentlemen were only investigating and I wasn't clear what they were investigating.'

Asked about the reference to the *Ironside* programme, McTavish explained that she and her colleagues were chatting about television and she had said she liked the programme. 'They asked me if I had seen the one about the geriatric ward sister who was doing in all the old dears for their money. I said I hadn't because I had been on the backshift that night.'

Sister McTavish said she was 'completely shattered' when she was cautioned by the police.

Cross-examined by the Solicitor-General, McTavish said she was very angry when Dr Saxena did not come to her ward to see Mrs Devine. She agreed the doctor did not have her experience but she had taken instructions from him to inject a dangerous drug at her suggestion.

On the final day of evidence in the third week of her trial, Jessie McTavish told the court in no uncertain manner: 'I am a very God-fearing person. I do not believe in euthanasia, regardless of the circumstances. I would certainly not kill a patient, especially an elderly woman who was placed in my care. I would certainly not take on myself on God's earth to inject any person with insulin. The Crown is wrong. I am a caring nurse and I do not believe in euthanasia or endangering the life of any person in my care.'

The Solicitor-General said: 'You had borrowed 900 units of insulin. So there should have been at least 900 units in the ward. You have heard the evidence that there was none.'

'That's correct.'

The Solicitor-General then said, 'If your story is correct then somebody must have removed it?'

'That's correct.'

Asked if she had any medical authority for injecting sterile water, McTavish replied, 'I was using my previous experience and I had seen Dr Ram Saxena and he told me to do what I liked.'

'Are you suggesting you had a blanket medical authority from Dr Saxena to inject whatever you liked and anything you liked?'

'I am.'

McTavish agreed she had no written authority to inject anyone but denied it was a breach of the rules to inject three patients without another nurse being present. Injections had to be recorded but not in the case of sterile water. She admitted giving 10 or 11 injections but a nurse was not always available to be with her.

She said she had authority from Dr Ram Saxena for certain injections and for others a blanket authority from Dr Judge. She gave Mrs Rowan a placebo to reassure her because she had not seen a doctor. Asked if the patient was agitating for a doctor's visit on a Saturday evening, she retorted, 'It's not unusual if you haven't seen a doctor for a month.' She had reported Dr Saxena to her nursing officer, as she was concerned that he was not coming to see her patients. She denied telling her lawyers that Dr Saxena was 'moonlighting' – acting as a locum when he was supposed to be on duty.

She also strongly denied saying she was on the verge of a nervous breakdown at the time or that her conduct was 'odd' in a number of ways. She said the love letter she wrote and crumpled up was 'straight out of *Women's Own*'.

She also denied ever seeing police notebooks before the trial containing her alleged statements that she gave insulin to Mrs Lyon because the patient wanted to be put out of her pain and misery.

When Mr McCluskey rose to address the jury after the evidence ended, he said the Crown's case did not depend on the scientific evidence alone. There was abundant circumstantial evidence to show that syringes were used to inject patients, that these injections produced symptoms of insulin and that insulin was borrowed by Sister McTavish and had disappeared.

It had been suggested by the defence, Mr McCluskey said, that Jessie McTavish obtained and acted on 'the most bizarre instructions' which history would ever record, given by a doctor to a ward sister — a blanket authority to inject 'all and sundry' as the sister saw fit. McCluskey countered this suggestion:

Can you really believe that this doctor gave such authority to a nurse he had never met before? Regardless of Dr Saxena's credibility, her story simply won't stand up. It won't do. Do you really think, in the circumstances she describes, she started to treat all those patients herself? No, in my submission, not at all.

In my submission, there can be no doubt and no room for doubt that these patients were injected without medical authority or prescription or necessity of medical treatment. The crucial things were — was insulin injected and did Mrs Lyon's death result from insulin poisoning?

Mr McCluskey reminded the jury that altogether 900 units of insulin had disappeared and argued that there was abundant evidence to show that it had been given to McTavish's patients. Some were very lucky to survive; Mrs Lyon received a dose which was lethal. The hypothesis of 'a mysterious injector' and 'a mysterious disposer of used syringes' in the ward was unacceptable: 'One can stretch credulity so far.'

The case, he said, was an important and in some ways a dramatic one. It was certainly tragic, whatever the result. For no one was it more important and tragic than for the accused herself. Her liberty was at stake. If she was guilty, the tragedy was obvious. If she was not guilty, the tragedy was hardly less clear.

The question was not whether the treatment was correct or misguided but if it was genuine medical treatment. Whether it was good, bad or indifferent was neither here nor there because there must be on the part of the person accused a wicked intention. There were massive contradictions between Sister McTavish's account of events and the vast body of evidence. Her failure to make entries in hospital records and indeed, the making of false entries, was a matter for which she could offer no explanation at all.

Was it not bizarre in the extreme that on the Sunday night when she was repeatedly predicting the death of a patient, she went on injecting that night and the next day? She gave a series of 13 injections and said she was giving sterile water as a placebo. But could you really believe she embarked on the administration of sterile water on such a massive scale without any entries in the records?

The Crown, he said, was not required to prove motive and he asked the jury to consider instead whether there was something that marked Sister McTavish as different. People working with her, after all, had noticed she was suddenly behaving oddly. He concluded:

> This was a woman who had been a nurse for many years, who had administered practically no injections for many months, who suddenly injected five patients at least a dozen times. When people say she was odd, unusual and that they didn't know what she was going to do next, it all adds up to a picture of something which had gone wrong. What it was, one cannot tell.

In an impressive and powerful closing speech to the jury, Mr Robertson, for the defence, said all the evidence showed Jessie McTavish was a nurse who never exhibited the slightest indication of malice, harassment, exasperation or the slightest indifference to her patients.

> She gave them flowers, she took them for bus runs, she even went to the funeral of a patient at the invitation of the woman's daughter. What kind of woman was this that the Crown claim deliberately and maliciously went about injuring patients? What possible reason or motive could a sister like Jessie McTavish have for doing what the Crown alleges she has done?
>
> It is said she predicted on various occasions that a patient was going to die. It is perfectly common in hospitals to talk of patients who are going to die. It is part of everyday life, unfortunately. Nurses in that situation do get used to it.

Comments such as 'Burke and Hare' and 'Doctor likes them to go quietly' and her supposed 'glazed eyes' were not evidence from which the jury could draw any conclusions, Mr Robertson argued. They might have been very good headlines in the Press but it was the kind of evidence from which no conclusions could be drawn in a serious criminal trial.

He likened the Crown's case to 'a dry stane dyke' from which a number of foundation stones had been swept away. Dr Ram Saxena, whose evidence was crucial to the case, was not credible or reliable and Sister Wishart was a proven liar.

What was left? Only scientific evidence — but here there was conflict among the experts. But it was Dr Ram Saxena who was the principal figure in 'this whole unhappy affair'. Jessie

McTavish said he was not interested in elderly people and that he said they would die anyway. He also told her she was an experienced nurse and she could give the patients what she liked.

> The Crown has suggested that no doctor would say this. You saw Dr Saxena in the witness box and you may think that is exactly the sort of thing he would say. That is exactly the kind of attitude he would have. Plainly, he did not have much concern for his job in the hospital. He was out doing those other jobs when he was on call and he was giving bottles of sherry to the telephonists.
>
> Here is a sister, a caring and concerned nurse for her patients, with a doctor who does not care tuppence, who could not care less about the patients and who has no interest in geriatrics, telling her to get on with it.

Despite some evidence to the contrary, Mr Robertson told the jury, sterile water was given to patients. Sister McTavish had given it at another hospital and understood it to be perfectly acceptable. None of the syringes found was of the kind that could be used for insulin. That was another flaw in the dry stane dyke.

Sister Wishart, he siad, was 'an odd and malevolent person'. She certainly did not spread goodwill and was forever reporting people and getting people into trouble. It was quite plain, he said, that somebody else had been borrowing or handling or lending insulin. Was that not very strange indeed? The whole argument for the Crown was that Jessie McTavish and no one else got insulin but the jury had heard the evidence of the borrowing that went on in the hospital. The Crown suggested she was the only one handling insulin but a piece of notepaper in someone else's handwriting referring to 40 units of insulin was found in a disposal bag. Where did that come from? Mr Robertson considered this evidence to prove that there was someone else handling insulin around that time.

Lord Robertson, in his summing up, said that there were seven heads in the Crown case. 1. No cause of death was found but Mrs Lyon had injection marks on her arm; 2. Tests at the Wellcome Foundation showed the presence of insulin in tissue; 3. A lethal dose was injected some time before her death; 4. Experts certified her death was due to insulin poisoning; 5.

The accused gave her an injection on June 30 and earlier acquired insulin although she had no diabetic patients; 6. The actions of Jessie McTavish, including statements which aroused suspicions she had done something to precipitate Mrs Lyon's illness; 7. Her subsequent conduct and statements to the police and to others.

Stated in this way, he told the jury, the Crown case might be considered to be a formidable one — as the Solicitor-General had said, 'an interlocking dyke or chain'. But even the strongest chain might have a weak link.

Of course we know there was a habit of borrowing and lending drugs, so it may well be that the stock which disappeared was quite properly and legitimately used by someone else. The Crown asked why the accused, on a Saturday afternoon, after the pharmacy had closed, and four days after she had got a stock on an emergency indent, required that amount of insulin in an emergency. Her answer was that the stock she got on the Wednesday was missing and she obtained new stocks because she had diabetic patients coming into the ward the following week.

This is a matter which you may consider of some importance. The Crown suggested that if that was the true explanation, why did she not say so the following day and why did she not produce evidence from witnesses who could have said that there were two patients coming in a day or two? Furthermore, if there was no need to use insulin in Ward 5 from the end of May, when the last diabetic patient left, to the last week in June, one question would of course at once occur: What happened to the sizeable quantity of insulin that was left?

Lord Robertson reminded the jury that it was not necessary for the Crown to prove a motive for the murder. It was, however, vital to prove 'wicked intent' on the part of Jessie McTavish. It would be no defence for her to say, 'I killed someone but it ws a mercy killing.' If that were permissible, he said, 'The world would be a very dangerous place.'

Pointedly, Lord Robertson said that while there was some evidence of unusual behaviour, it had not been suggested that there was any question of insanity of which the law should take note.

It had been one of the longest murder trials in Scotland for many years and no one envied the task of the eight men and seven women on the jury as they settled down to consider the complex evidence they had heard over the course of three weeks. They returned to a hushed High Court after almost four hours of deliberation to announce a majority verdict of guilty of murder.

Also by a majority, the jury found Jessie McTavish guilty of assaulting two other patients, Mrs Logan and Mrs Rowan, by injecting them with insulin and of assaulting Mrs Devine by injecting her with pethidine. They unanimously found her not guilty of assaulting a fifth patient, Mrs Margaret Ward, by injecting insulin.

Lord Robertson admonished Sister McTavish on the three charges of assault and sentenced her to life imprisonment for the murder.

There were cries of 'Oh, my God, no!' as the sentence was passed. Jessie McTavish, her head bowed, burst into tears. As she was led away, she said, 'I never did that . . . I never did anything like that.'

As newspapers at the time pointed out, the unthinkable had happened: an angel of mercy, dedicated by her calling to care for the sick, had been convicted of murdering a patient in her charge.

Under its chairman, Mr Simpson Stevenson, Greater Glasgow Health Board immediately set up an inquiry into the hospital. Mr Stevenson said the evidence in the trial had revealed a number of disquieting features, which included doctors taking private locum work while employed in the hospital; doctors signing death certificates without examining bodies; and drugs going missing from wards.

Various administrative procedures practised at Ruchill also came under scrutiny and, as Mr Stevenson said, the lesson learned at Ruchill would be a yardstick for all hospitals. However, none of this explained what possible bizarre and abrupt disintegration of personality turned a capable, concerned and respected nurse into a woman found guilty of murdering a patient.

A nurse who trained with Sister McTavish at Ruchill, Staff Nurse Shenna Welsh, said afterwards, 'There was no one in our year who was prouder than Jay to put on that nurse's uniform.' Sister Aileen Bryce said Jay was 'full of confidence, personality and fun' and acknowledged by everyone as 'a good nurse'.

One of the senior detectives on the case referred to 'one mad week in June when a nursing sister decided to play God', but according to doctors and nurses who had worked with her McTavish was a dedicated nurse. She loved life, they said, and adored her hobby of salmon fishing. When she was freed after the initial assault charge, Jessie McTavish said: 'When you think about it, I have spent all my life saving life. My hospital badge says 'Protect and Sustain'. That is what I have tried to live up to.'

But at the end of the trial, it was revealed that although Jessie McTavish was in fact dedicated to her profession and had won coveted prizes while qualifying as a general nurse, a fever nurse and a state registered midwife, she had suffered a nervous breakdown when she was jilted by a man in Canada six years earlier and had spent eight months in a mental hospital after trying to kill herself.

Her mother, Mrs Mary McTavish, said: 'From the time she was a little girl she never wanted to be anything else but a nurse. There's no bad in that girl and as long as I live I will never believe she did these things to these old women.'

Jessie's family were determined to fight on to clear her name and an immediate appeal was lodged. Early in December 1974, she was granted leave to appeal.

McTavish appealed on six grounds, three of them involving misdirection of the jury by the presiding judge. Because the three judges in the Court of Criminal Appeal called for the full notes of the evidence, the appeal was not heard until February the following year.

Her counsel, Mr Donald Robertson, told the appeal court that the trial judge failed to give equal prominence to the defence case and wrongly admitted police evidence relating to the replies she was alleged to have made when charged with assault. Mr Robertson argued that when McTavish was charged with assault the victim was already dead; she was therefore entitled to assume that assault would be the only charge against her. He also submitted that the judge had erred in telling the jury that there was no dispute about the accused having made statements about giving a patient insulin; it was 'a fatal failure' on his part to omit to draw their attention specifically to the fact that the accused denied making the statements.

Mr Robertson also claimed that the judge rehearsed the Crown case in great detail but gave the defence case only a brief summary.

The Solicitor-General, however, maintained that the alleged statements were not the most crucial evidence. There were people who saw things being done and there was a vast amount of evidence other than the statements.

There was cheering and loud applause in the court on 31 January 1975 when the Court of Criminal Appeal unanimously quashed the murder conviction. Jessie McTavish, who had sat between two prison officers with her head bowed, listened intently to the 20-minute judgement and then wept as she was led from the court to freedom.

Lord Wheatley, the Lord Justice Clerk, who presided with Lords Kissen and Thomson, said the second ground of appeal was that the judge misdirected the jury in regard to the police evidence and McTavish's replies upon being charged. The judge referred the jury to the replies only in the context of whether they had been elicited fairly and failed to put the fact that she denied altogether making the replies. It was also claimed he failed adequately to direct the jury on the value of the police evidence.

According to the police witnesses her first reply to the charge was: 'I gave a half c.c. of insulin soluble to Mrs Lyon only because she wanted to be put out of her pain and misery.'

Her second alleged reply was: 'I gave Mrs Lyon a half c.c. of soluble insulin. She was taking a cerebral and she wanted out of her misery.'

The appeal judges claimed that Lord Robertson made no reference whatsoever to McTavish's denial of the police allegations and that this was highly prejudicial and constituted a misdirection in law:

> We have given careful and anxious consideration to the judge's charge. At the end of 13 days of evidence in a highly complicated trial, it was a far from easy task for the judge to give a comprehensive and clearly defined charge to the jury.
>
> In our opinion, but for a single omission, which a few words could have cured, it was a well constructed, clear and accurate charge.
>
> It is not disputed that he failed to direct the jury specifically to

consider whether she had made the statements attributed to her by the police which, if accepted, were vital pieces of evidence of a highly incriminating nature.

On the authority of a murder case in 1935, such a failure would be fatal to the conviction. In both cases, there was ample evidence to warrant the conviction and, in both cases, the statements were taken as accurate whereas the accused's version was a declaration of innocence. Nothing could be more vital.

Even the most experienced judge may fail to give a direction which ought to have been given, particularly at the end of a long and exhausting trial. The judge here failed to give such a direction and failed to draw the attention of the jury to her version of the replies she gave.

We are unable to find in the charge as a whole, or in any of the selected passages, sufficient to repair that deficiency by inference or implication.

The question was whether the omission was sufficiently material to vitiate the verdict. The answer to that could only be that it was.

A passage by Lord Aitchison in the 1935 case had expressed similar feelings: 'I reach this conclusion with regret. It can never be a light thing to interfere with the verdict of a jury on a charge of murder and, as I have already said, there is in my view, ample evidence to support the verdict.'

After saying it was the appeal court's plain duty to set the verdict aside, Lord Wheatley quashed the conviction and sentence and told Jessie McTavish, 'You are free to go.'

Afterwards, elated with the verdict, McTavish said: 'I could never quite believe that the system of justice in this country would let me down. I have received 1,000 letters and 106 Christmas cards in prison all supporting me.'

As she celebrated with her mother and three brothers, her lawyer, who had spent 20 months on her case, and Sister Aileen Bryce, who had gone out on a limb in her evidence to support her, Jessie said: 'I had a strange dream last Sunday night. I dreamed that another prisoner would have her sentence halved at her appeal and that I would walk out of the court free. Both dreams came true.'

Inadvertently, Jessie McTavish became the champion of euthanasia by virtue of this *cause célèbre*, even though her defence all along had been innocence and she had never pleaded euthanasia. Enjoying her freedom, she still renounced her unwelcome reputation: 'I have never believed in euthanasia. I have never practised it and I never will.'

On Scottish Television later that night, she said: 'I have been a scapegoat — to carry the can. Mrs Lyon's death cost me eight months in prison. I know I gave her sterile water.'

Just before the end of the trial Ward 5 was closed and the patients were rehoused in another geriatric ward. Preparations were made to turn the ward into a day centre. Circulars were sent out ordering nurses to distribute medicines in teams of two and every ward started a 'Drugs Borrowed' book with signatures and counter-signatures. Now, no one would hand out even Panadol without recording it in a treatment book. More trained night staff were introduced.

Despite the indifference of the junior doctors and the frustrations and handicaps in running a geriatric ward, there is no doubt Jessie McTavish ran a happy and successful ward until that fateful, curious week in June 1973. Many people who worked with her were unequivocal in their loyalty to her.

One sister summed it all up when she said: 'When Jay took over the ward most of the patients were bedridden. And she got most of them on their feet.'

Jessie McTavish herself, speaking without bitterness, said she thought nurses were asked to accept too much responsibility. Ruchill was not typical of other hospitals she had known but it was the worst. The general indifference of the system there began to wear her down.

What went wrong? Perhaps all the deficiencies at the hospital go a long way to explain how she was forced to assume an undesirable degree of responsibility for her patients and the unhappy consequences that followed.

CHAPTER 9
Love and Lust

When young Sheila Watson married Maxwell Garvie, a handsome wealthy young farmer, in 1955, it was a childhood dream come true for her.

For three years until she was 15 she had lived on the Royal estate at Balmoral, where her father was a stonemason. When she was 13, she had played the part of Queen Victoria in a pageant at Aboyne Castle in the presence of members of the Royal Family. When she left school she worked for a time at a telephone exchange, returning to Balmoral as a maid. Her family later left Balmoral to live in Stonehaven and Sheila then worked as a clerk for a bus company.

She met Max Garvie, who was then 21, at a summer dance in the local town hall and they fell deeply in love. Within a year they were married and the lifestyle she had gazed at enviously at Balmoral became a reality for her. Sheila loved the life at their farmhouse at West Cairnbeg, Fordoun, Kincardineshire, where she and her husband had three cars, maids and a private plane.

For many years they were blissfully happy. But in the early 1960s a cloud arose, growing into a storm that engulfed Max Garvie, the brilliant young man with everything that life could offer.

It was later said that Garvie underwent a change of personality and began a course of conduct which eventually led to his death. There were claims that he set up his own permissive society and created 'a Frankenstein monster which eventually rose up and slew him'. He became a Jekyll-and-Hyde character — one moment the fine, decent, handsome husband and the next an evil personality.

He started to drink more and more and took pills. Sometimes he was elated and at other times depressed and his attitude to his wife and family changed. He told his mother-in-law he wanted 'kicks' out of life.

When he disappeared on the night of 14 May 1968, Garvie

147

was not immediately reported missing by his wife. Sheila told her three children before they left for school the next day that their father had gone to Edinburgh, but she confided to her 59-year-old mother, Mrs Edith Watson, that her husband would 'not come back'. Her mother said, 'You don't mean he's dead, do you?' and Sheila nodded.

Mrs Watson was stunned by the news but lived for three months with her deadly secret before going to the police. She felt she had to do something. She was convinced her daughter did not know where Max Garvie's body was and she kept silent to protect her daughter and her three grandchildren.

Mrs Watson was convinced also that Max Garvie's conduct had changed her daughter completely. She had been a decent and respectable girl who was very well thought of at Balmoral.

Mrs Watson's visit to the police led to the arrest of her daughter, who was then 33, Sheila's 22-year-old lover, Brian Tevendale, and Tevendale's friend, 20-year-old Alan Peters from Fort Augustus. All three were accused of murdering Max Garvie by striking him on the head with the butt of a rifle or iron bar and then shooting him. The indictment further alleged that Tevendale had previously evinced malice and ill-will against Garvie.

All three denied murder and Mrs Garvie lodged a special defence incriminating one or other or both of the men. She also lodged a motion attacking her husband's character in respect of his 'unnatural and perverted sexual practices'.

Peters lodged a special defence blaming both Tevendale and Mrs Garvie for the murder and claiming that any acts by him in connection with the murder were committed under the coercion of Tevendale.

Mr Ewan Stewart, QC, the Solicitor-General, (later a judge) and Mr Hugh Morton (now a judge) appeared for the Crown. Mrs Garvie was represented by Mr Lionel Daiches, QC, the silver-tongued advocate who had appeared in many important criminal trials. Mr Kenneth Cameron, later to become Lord Advocate and now a High Court judge, appeared for Tevendale and Dr R.R. Taylor, QC, represented Peters.

The trial opened at the High Court in Aberdeen on 19 November 1968 and became the trial of the century as revelations of lust and sexual depravity unfolded.

The scene was set on the opening day of the trial when Mr Daiches referred to a special candle-lit room where music played while Max Garvie encouraged his wife to have intercourse with Tevendale.

Mr Daiches was cross-examining a Church of Scotland minister, the Rev Kenneth Thomson, of Fordoun Parish Church. The Garvies were both members of his congregation. The minister said Mrs Garvie had not told him anything about this special room but her mother, Mrs Watson, had told him that Max gave £100 to Tevendale to entertain Sheila.

Mr Thomson and his wife exchanged visits with the Garvies and he became very friendly with Max. They had an interest in common, as both became members of the Scottish National Party. Tevendale also attended meetings of the party but he did not see Tevendale in the company of the Garvies until the late summer of 1967.

The minister visited Max Garvie in October or November 1967 after Mrs Garvie left with the children to live in Stonehaven with Tevendale. He was asked to mediate and went to Stonehaven. Tevendale did not want Sheila to return to her husband but the minister's advice to her was to go back for the sake of the children.

Mrs Garvie returned to the farmhouse two or three days later. Her husband was drinking very heavily at the time because of the strain and told Mr Thomson that Tevendale had threatened to shoot him. Garvie also told him he had had an affair with Tevendale's sister, Mrs Trudy Birse, but had withdrawn from it as she was becoming emotionally involved.

Garvie wanted his wife to end her association with Tevendale. In the early spring of 1968 she left again but they were later reconciled. Mr Thomson said Mrs Garvie told him later she was physically ill-treated by her husband and that things were not happy between them.

Max Garvie disappeared in May and in August Mrs Garvie came to Mr Thomson's manse. She was distressed and said she was having 'a rough time' as far as public opinion was concerned. She spoke of her husband's sexual aberrations and of conversations they had had with a psychiatrist. She told him this was a side of Max he had never seen.

'I understood from what she said that she was subjected to a perverted form of sexual intercourse. She did imply that her husband had homosexual tendencies and I found this difficult to reconcile.'

The impression the minister got when he first knew the Garvies was that theirs was a perfectly normal, happy marriage. Mrs Garvie had told him, however, that her husband was interested in a nudist camp, although she did not say she had gone to such a place with him.

Asked by Mr Daiches if she had told him her husband had bought a cottage and had founded his own nudist club, Mr Thomson said she told him about the cottage and indicated something of this sort was taking place there, but he was not aware it was known locally as 'kinky cottage'. He was also not aware that Max Garvie had insisted on his wife ceremonially opening the club. He agreed there were aspects of Max Garvie's life he knew nothing about.

'Did Mr Garvie invite Tevendale to seduce his wife?' Mr Daiches asked.

'Mrs Garvie did not suggest that in as many words. She used a phrase that seemed to be indicative of it. She said Max was interested in Brian's performance.'

'Did Mrs Garvie ever tell you that Mr Garvie had arranged a special candle-lit room and arranged for music to be played and encouraged his wife to have intercourse with Tevendale?'

'No.'

'Did she ever tell you he gave £100 to Tevendale to entertain his wife?'

'I was told that by Mrs Garvie's mother.'

'Did she ever tell you the three of them went to bed together and performed the sexual act?'

'No.'

Mr Thomson said she spoke of them going out as a foursome and indicated that her husband encouraged her association with Tevendale. She gave him the impression that she and Tevendale had almost been thrown together. It also appeared to him that Max was sorry the situation had been allowed to develop and that, whether or not Max Garvie was to blame for what had happened in the past, by 1968 he had broken off his relationship with Tevendale's sister, Trudy, and wanted to continue with his marriage.

No sooner had Mrs Garvie's mother, Mrs Edith Watson, begun her evidence than she began to sob and collapsed in the witness box. She was carried from the court and completed her evidence next day.

She said her daughter's marriage was at first happy but 18 months ago something had gone wrong. Max started bringing Tevendale to the house but she had no suspicions about her daughter and Tevendale. She was later told they were associating.

Her daughter told her on August 15 that Max had disappeared. Sheila said one of their three cars had gone when she came downstairs. Her husband had come home late and when she woke up, he had gone.

Mrs Watson said she went to the farm next day, where she had a conversation with her daughter about Max's disappearance. Sheila told her 'You will have no worries. He won't come back.'

Mrs Watson said to her daughter, 'You don't mean he's dead, do you?' Her daughter simply nodded her head.

'I said, "Oh, the poor beggar." I felt so shocked and stunned. I asked if he had suffered and she said "No". The word murder was never used in the conversation.'

The next day she questioned her daughter about her husband's death and asked what she would do if anything happened and the police came. Sheila said, 'I will fight because I am innocent.' Her daughter never spoke about the location of the body, and Mrs Watson thought that she did not in fact know where it was.

After the disappearance of Max, her daughter did not go to the police. She continued to see Tevendale and spent three nights a week in Aberdeen away from the farm, leaving the telephone number of Tevendale's sister for any emergency. Mrs Watson said she tried to point out it was wrong to continue to see Tevendale.

On August 14, her daughter phoned to say she was bringing Tevendale for tea. Mrs Watson objected, but Sheila said she would run her own life and would please herself.

Mrs Watson said she decided to go to the police, because Max had told her that if anything ever happened to him to look after the children and see they did not come into contact with Tevendale. 'I realised I would have to tell the police and that meant involving my daughter. I felt I had to do something.'

Next morning, she told her daughter what she intended to do and then left the house. She met the farm grieve, who took her to his home and gave her a cup of tea. Then he drove her to the police.

Cross-examined, Mrs Watson said that for the first ten years the marriage had been really happy. Then she noticed a change in her son-in-law. He was drinking more and taking Pro-Plus pills. Sometimes he was elated and sometimes depressed. His attitude towards his wife and family changed. She knew this was not the real Max Garvie.

She agreed he had become a Jekyll-and-Hyde character. One time she found her daughter in tears and Sheila tried to tell her of the intimate side of her marriage. But when her daughter saw that she did not understand what she was trying to tell her, she stopped.

Max told Mrs Watson he wanted kicks out of life. She first met Tevendale when Max brought him to the house. Then a situation developed in 1967 which resulted in Max becoming friendly with Tevendale's sister. Max and Trudy Birse became lovers and her daughter told her at that time that Max had 'thrown her' at Tevendale.

Asked if Max was perfectly happy for his wife to make love to Tevendale provided it was for kicks, but became jealous and upset when a deeper emotion developed, Mrs Watson said, 'Yes, that was the position.'

Max had told her that when the four of them were together at the farm or at hotels, he had intercouse with Mrs Birse while his wife had intercourse with Tevendale. This conduct changed her daughter completely. Before that she had been a decent girl.

A meeting was arranged in December 1967 in Mrs Watson's home because she and her husband were anxious to break up this foursome and effect a reconciliation between her daughter and Max Garvie. At the meeting, her daughter and Max agreed to such a course. Mrs Birse and Tevendale were also there. Mrs Birse said that she could cope with Max's sexual demands when Sheila could not. Mrs Watson understood that

Max had been making certain sexual demands which her daughter thought were unnatural.

Mrs Watson said she got the impression Max wanted his wife to get involved with Tevendale, but not for ever. She thought he got some kind of twisted kick out of imagining his wife being made love to by Tevendale. Max Garvie had mentioned this to her. He wanted his wife to have a good time and did not care who she slept with as long as she always returned to him. Mrs Watson told him that was not her idea of a happy marriage.

'Did he ever tell you that on one occasion he insisted that he and Tevendale should go to bed with Mrs Garvie?'

'He said he had tossed a coin to see who would sleep with my daughter first. It was horrible . . . I can't go on . . .'

Mrs Watson then testified that this situation had a terrible effect on her daughter and she had thought Sheila was on the verge of a nervous breakdown.

Events leading to the finding of the decomposed body of Max Garvie in a tunnel at a disused quarry at St Cyrus, near Montrose, three months after he disappeared, were described on the second day of the trial.

Farmer Kenneth Thomson said the disused quarry was near his home. One morning, in the middle of May, he was awakened at 5 a.m. and saw a cattle float outside. The driver asked the way to Lauriston Castle nearby. Thomson directed him and went back to bed.

Half an hour later, he was awakened again when his doorbell rang. Two men told him their car was stuck and asked for a tow. He recognised Tevendale, whose father owned the Bush Hotel at St Cyrus. Tevendale had lived there as a boy. He identified the other man as Peters.

He took his tractor and found their car ten yards inside the gateway to the quarry. Tevendale said they had got lost and had reversed there to turn. There was mud on their shoes but they did not seem flustered.

A few months later, on August 17, he helped the police open up a culvert in the quarry. In the tunnel they found the decomposed body of Max Garvie.

Death was due to a gunshot wound in the neck which had fractured the skull. The bullet hole was just behind the right ear. Dr Douglas Bain, who had carried out the post-mortem, was then asked to look at the skull of Max Garvie, which was handed to him in a cardboard box. Asked to demonstrate where the bullet had fractured the skull, Dr Bain took out the yellowing skull and held it up towards the jury, indicating the direction the bullet had taken.

Turning white, Sheila Garvie quickly looked away when the skull was produced. Mr Daiches told the court she was feeling indisposed and asked for an adjournment. The skull was not produced again when the court resumed.

Max Garvie's solicitor told the court his estate was worth about £48,000. Four insurance policies worth £55,000 payable to Mrs Garvie would not be paid unless the insurance companies were satisfied with regard to the circumstances of his death. After her husband disappeared he prepared a will for Mrs Garvie but there was no mention of her husband in it.

When Tevendale's 31-year-old sister, Trudy Birse, a tall ash blonde, entered the witness box, the judge, Lord Thomson, warned her that she need not answer any questions inferring she had committed adultery.

She said she had married in 1957 and her husband Alfred had been until recently a constable in Aberdeen City Police. Her brother Brian first became friendly with the Garvies in April 1967 and she met Max Garvie in August that year when he and his wife visited her mother's house. She could see her brother and Sheila were very friendly. 'I was attracted to Max on the first occasion we met. He said he had been attracted to me.'

Arrangements were made for her and her husband and family to go to the airstrip at Fordoun one Sunday. She went for a flight in Max's two-seater plane. While they were flying he asked her if he could see her again. From then she started to see a lot of Max. Sometimes she went out alone with him and other times as a foursome with her brother and Sheila. The four of them went out for drinks to hotels in and around Aberdeen. When Max was out with her alone, Brian and Sheila were allowed to be together.

She had also gone to the farm at West Cairnbeg and stayed the night there and had intercourse with Max. Her brother and Sheila were also together. On one occasion when they went to

Edinburgh she and Max were at the Minto Hotel and Sheila and Brian were at the County Hotel.

> Max encouraged the friendship between Sheila and Brian. In fact he nourished it. He told me Sheila was frigid and did not respond to his love-making in the way he wanted her. He was encouraging the friendship so that Sheila would be a better lover for him. He didn't want her to go away with any other man permanently. Because of his position he did not want any emotions involved. He did not want the marriage to end but in my view he was not doing anything to save it.

At Cairnbeg she saw books on sexual technique. Max told her he had read them. Asked if Max continued to have sexual relations with his wife while he was having a relationship with her, Mrs Birse said sometimes at six o'clock in the morning he would tell her to get out of his bed and ask for Sheila to come through to him. Mrs Birse would go to a spare room while Max expected his wife, after having been all night with Brian, to go through and have sex with him. Sheila did not like it.

After a while, a feeling of strain developed and a meeting was held at Cairnbeg during which Brian and Sheila both said they were in love with each other. Sheila told Max he could not expect anything else from the way he had encouraged and helped their friendship along. 'She said he had used us, including myself, for his own selfish ends and couldn't expect her to give up Brian just like that.'

Later, there was another conference at the home of Mrs Watson, who told her and Brian to leave the house and not to see Max and Sheila again because it was all over. Trudy stopped seeing Max but Sheila and her brother continued to see one another. Max was very angry at their continued association and threatened to shoot Sheila between the eyes.

Later Sheila phoned and said she could not stand the situation any longer. Trudy drove Sheila and Brian to Bradford, but they returned after a short time. In her house she heard Sheila and Brian talking about Max and heard them say jokingly that 'Max would have to go.'

On the night of May 14–15 Brian and Peters went out together. Her husband was on shift work and she went to bed at 11.30 p.m. Next morning her husband was in bed as it was his day off. When she went downstairs she found her brother sitting in the living room. There was a pile of clothing on the kitchen floor. When she asked him what he had been up to, he replied: 'It's nothing to do with you. Just mind your own business.'

She sensed there was something wrong as he was very quiet. She kept on at him and he then said, 'It's been done. It's over,' or words to that effect. She asked him what he meant and he just looked at her. She asked him again and he said, 'Max . . . he's dead.'

Mrs Birse began to sob but continued her evidence in a voice scarcely above a whisper. 'I was very upset and went upstairs to the bathroom. I didn't want my children to see me upset so I controlled myself and went downstairs.' Her brother left without saying anything more. Later that morning she washed the clothes lying in the kitchen.

Brian later told her Sheila had let him and Peters into the farmhouse. He said Sheila told them that Max was asleep and they went through to the room. After a little hesitation, her brother said Peters struck Max with a steel bar. Brian honestly believed Max was already dead when he shot him. The explanation did not satisfy her. What concerned her was whether Max had suffered.

While she was doing the washing, which included a boiler suit, jeans, shirt, socks and tee-shirts, she got a phone call from Sheila. She asked if she could come to see her and arrived a quarter of an hour later.

'She was upset. Were looking at one another, not saying anything to begin with. She asked me if Brian had told me anything about Max and I said "Just a little." She was shaking a bit and I told her to sit down and I made her a cup of tea.'

Sheila then said: 'It had to be done. I couldn't take it any more. There was no other way.'

She went with Sheila in her car to where Brian was working. They all went to a hotel. 'I got up and went to the toilet, leaving them alone. I thought I should not be there. I felt they wanted to be together. They were holding hands and spoke as if to keep me out of the conversation.'

Sheila then drove them to the bar where Brian worked and dropped him off. On the way back, Sheila spoke to her about a mattress that had been messed up and soiled and said she was trying to replace it without attracting attention.

That night Sheila phoned from Cairnbeg. She was in a terrible state, crying and upset. She asked her to come down to the farm and Trudy said she would try to come down later.

In another phone call later the same evening, she spoke to Sheila about the mattress. She and her husband had a mattress which was too short; later, she and Brian took it to Cairnbeg. They arranged to phone when they were near the farm in case Sheila's mother or brother was there. Sheila wanted them to arrive at the farm unseen. They drove straight into the garage and took in the mattress. Brian and Sheila took it upstairs. Brian and Sheila tied up a mattress in the bedroom and brought it back to the Birses' house. By then it was four o'clock in the morning. Brian and Alfred Birse took the mattress to a dump and burned it. Trudy had already told her husband all that Brian had said that morning about the killing.

Sheila brought a plastic bag with some clothing in it to her house. She learned later it was the clothing Max was wearing when he disappeared. Sheila asked her to burn it. She didn't want to burn anything at Cairnbeg as she didn't want to draw attention. Mrs Birse said she burned the clothing in the back garden, assisted by her husband. Sheila paid her £18 for the mattress.

She said Peters and Brian worked in the same garage and did 'homers', going out mending people's cars. Peters came to the house quite a lot. On July 26, after Max had disappeared, Peters was married. Brian and Sheila were witnesses. The reception was held in her home in Aberdeen and Sheila cooked a turkey. Sheila told her she had given Alan Peters £5 as a wedding present.

Peters, she said, had nothing to do with the foursome and she had never seen him at the farm. Cross-examined by Mr Daiches, for Sheila Garvie, Mrs Birse agreed that Max Garvie was 'a man of magnetic personality'. Her relationship with him had developed fairly quickly. While she was on the flight with Max they arranged to meet and after that the four of them had a social evening at Bucksburn. Max came to her house the next day. They had half a bottle of vodka and some other drinks. That was the first time he made love to her and it was the start of their relationship. On another occasion, he drove her home and made love to her.

She and her husband were invited to a party at West Cairnbeg. Max, Sheila and Brian were also there. They went out to hotels for some drinks and everybody was 'paired' off except her husband.

In one hotel, where Max knew the manager, he arranged for a girl to come back to the farm with them. The girl was supposed to be 'a blind date' for her husband.

'Had Max the idea that you would accommodate him, Sheila would attend to Brian and your husband would be looked after by this girl who was a blind date? This was now a sextet?' asked Mr Daiches.

Mrs Birse answered: 'It seems that way. My husband was not too keen on the blind date idea. It was Max's idea to get the girl for my husband.' Asked what happened when they got back to the farm, she replied: 'When we first arrived, Max lit candles in the room and put on soft romantic music and encouraged us to dance. Sheila and Brian were dancing together. Max was dancing with me and my husband and this girl were sitting in two separate armchairs.'

'Your husband's attitude to this kind of thing was a little more conservative than yours?'

'Yes. The evening wore on. We had more drinks, then Sheila and Brian went upstairs. Max and I left and went upstairs, leaving my husband and this girl in the living room. The music was still playing. I didn't see my husband until the following morning.'

'What did your husband, a serving police officer, think of all this?'

'I knew what was in Max's mind about the party. My husband and I had a long discussion, a detailed discussion before the party. I tried to explain the deep feelings I had for Max. He tried to understand my feelings. I had fallen for Max. My husband was not too keen to go to the party in the first place.'

'It must have been perfectly apparent, with romantic music and candlelight, that Sheila and Brian had not gone upstairs to discuss philosophy and that you and Max went upstairs in order to go to bed with each other?'

'Two days earlier I had warned my husband that this could happen.'

'He was left with romantic music playing and the candlelight guttering . . . left alone with a blind date?'

'Yes.'

'Not everyone could have been as understanding as your husband?'

'That is very true.'

Mrs Birse testified that it did not matter to Max that he was committing adultery and that his wife was committing adultery, provided there was no emotional relationship. He got some kind of kick or thrill from the fact that his wife was having a love affair and some sort of satisfaction out of hearing about the methods and reactions of Sheila and Brian in their lovemaking.

Asked if Max asked her to find out those details from Brian, Mrs Birse said, 'And from Sheila.' Max asked her the most intimate details of his wife's relationship. He said he told Sheila that he had got more pleasure out of her in two weeks than he had all his married life.

'I think it was a very cruel thing to say to his wife. He showed me photogrphs of Sheila in the nude, taken at Cairnbeg and on beaches. He also showed me pornographic pictures and pictures taken at nudist camps.' She identified a folder of nude pictures of Sheila taken by Max.

Max spoke to her about certain things to which his wife was reluctant to accede. Max considered it to be a normal part of marriage but they were homosexual demands.

Later, she noticed some peculiarities in Max's behaviour. He seemed a quite normal and happy person but he always ordered doubles at bars on every occasion. One night when Brian was driving them in Max's Jaguar after the foursome had been out drinking, Max opened the car door and put his fingers on the road and burned his hand. She tried to hold on to him but he turned round and said, 'Stop being so childish.'

'He was very friendly with Brian. He told me he actually loved Brian more than his wife. I found it quite strange that he should say such a thing.'

She spoke of occasions when she was unable to join the foursome. To decide who was going to sleep with Sheila, Max and Brian tossed a coin — the best of three. Max lost and on the next occasion, he insisted on the three of them, Max, Sheila and Brian, sleeping together.

When Max broke off the relationship with her, he told her he had no feelings for her. She was very upset. The reason their relationship stopped was because Brian and Sheila had feelings for one another. Max knew at any time he felt like it he could stop but he could not control his wife's relationship.

When she was questioned about what Brian and Sheila told her after the murder, Mrs Birse began to sob and shake.

'It was not easy for me to accept that Max was dead. We were all friends; then Max started his strange ways. I naturally did not go along with what happened to Max. It was the most dreadful thing to happen to anyone.'

The next witness was her husband, 33-year-old Alfred Birse, who was by then a former member of Aberdeen Police Force. He said he was aware his wife was going away from time to time with Garvie and sometimes with Brian and Sheila. After his wife and Max broke off their relationship, Brian and Sheila continued to meet and the situation became increasingly difficult.

Brian had once said jokingly that he would have to take action to get Max 'out of the way'. He mentioned trying to arrange an accident to Max's car or his plane. The plane was to be blown up by remote control. Brian blamed Max for having him banned from a hotel and for arranging for two young men to way-lay him in Aberdeen one night with the object of beating him up. Brian had managed to escape.

On the morning of May 15, Alfred Birse was still in bed when his wife told him something distressing concerning Brian. She was very upset. Brian gave him a pair of boots and a rucksack and asked him to destroy them. That night, Trudy and Brian went to Cairnbeg with the mattress from his bed. He slept in the living room that night.

During the night another mattress was brought to his home. It was rolled up and tied and there were some articles of clothing. He and Brian took the mattress to a quarry and burned it. Later Sheila asked him his advice on how to clean fingerprints from a gun.

In cross-examination, Birse agreed that it had been apparent to him that a crime had been committed and that he did nothing about it and took a considerable part in concealing what might have been evidence. He also agreed that he kept

silent for three months while the police were searching for
Max, all the while knowing perfectly well Mr Garvie would
never come back. But he had nothing to do with the death or
disappearance of Max Garvie.

Mr Daiches asked: 'So although you had nothing to do with
it, for reasons that seemed good to you, you participated in a
plan to keep up the appearance that he had disappeared rather
than that he had been done away with?'

'Yes.'

Detective-Inspector James Murray said that when he
interviewed Mrs Garvie on May 31 about the disappearance she
said her husband had been to an SNP meeting at Stonehaven
and arrived home at 11.30 p.m. He had started drinking and
then they had an argument about sex. She took two sleeping
tablets and remembered nothing until the next morning, when
she awoke to find her husband had not been to bed. His car
was gone and was later found at the airstrip.

This was treated as a normal missing person's case and the
Detective-Inspector gave a circular to the *Police Gazette*. In
addition to Garvie's photograph, this included a description of
him and the clothing he was wearing. There was also
information about his character and habits, most of it coming
from Mrs Garvie. The words 'strong homosexual tendencies'
came partly from Mrs Garvie and partly from Tevendale. The
words 'a man of considerable wealth and until three or four
years ago was completely rational' came from Mrs Garvie, who
also gave him information about his nudist camp activities.

On August 16, Detective-Inspector Murray was told Mrs
Garvie's mother had made certain allegations at a police
station. He went to the farm and saw Mrs Garvie. He told her
certain allegations had been made and that he had reason to
believe Max Garvie had been murdered and that she was
involved. She replied, 'Well, that is not true.'

She accompanied him to the police station and he later told
her that her husband's body had been found. She said, 'How
was he killed?'

When she was charged with her husband's murder, she
replied, 'I did not shoot, kill or cause injury to my husband.'
Tevendale was also charged and the couple were allowed to be
together in a police office for a time. After they had both

appeared in chambers before a sheriff at Stonehaven, Mrs.
Garvie made a statement:

> I awakened with someone standing whispering to me to get up.
> The bedroom light was off but the room was lit from the light on
> the landing. I recognised the figure and the voice of Brian
> Tevendale. He took me by the arm out to the landing and standing
> there was a fair-haired young man. I didn't know who he was at all.
> I was hustled through to the bathroom and told to get in and stay
> there. I noticed Brian was carrying a gun. I didn't know at that
> time that it belonged to Max.
>
> I heard our bedroom door closing and terrible thumping noises.
> About five minutes later, Brian came through and tried the handle
> but I had it locked. I opened the door. He said something like 'You
> won't have any more of him to put up with' and asked me to stay
> beside the girls' door in case they came out.
>
> The two of them were a while in the bedroom and they were
> pulling Max out in a groundsheet type of thing. I can't remember
> whether they took sheets with them or not because I was terribly
> upset — in a hell of a state — but I do remember they weren't long
> in going away.

She said Brian phoned the next day and said they had left
Max's clothes in the garage. She became distressed on the
phone and Brian told her to take the clothes to Trudy and she
would get rid of them.

'He told me the night before if I squealed he would get me
involved and get about 25 years in prison.' When she asked
him how he was going to get away with it, he said he was going
to hide the body. She asked him where but he said he would
not tell her.

Peters also made a statement in which he said:

> He brought it up at work a few weeks before. He just said he was
> wanting to get rid of the bloke and would I come with him so that
> he could have transport.
>
> We went to Cairnbeg and parked on a road at the rear of the
> farm. We went into the garage and Mrs Garvie let us into the
> house. Brian got the gun from the back of the door and we went
> through to the sitting room. We got a drink from Mrs Garvie then
> she showed us to the room upstairs.
>
> We waited there till Mr Garvie came home and went to bed.
> When he was asleep, his wife came through and told us. Then we
> went through and Brian hit him on the back of the head with the
> butt of the gun and then shot him. We tied him up in a plastic

groundsheet and took him down to the car. Then Brian took Max's car to the airfield and I followed.

Peters then described how they took Garvie's body to the old quarry, where he poured petrol on the groundsheet and burned it.

Sergeant Robert Grant, who was stationed at Laurencekirk, played an important part in the whole investigation. He had had deep suspicions about Max Garvie's disappearance. Max had come to see him in March to report his wife missing. He was most distressed and in tears. Later Garvie told him his wife had left Bradford for London; he said he would bring her home and start life again.

On May 11, in response to a call from Garvie's sister, Mrs Kerr, Sergeant Grant began inquiries into the disappearance. At that time Mrs Garvie had not reported her husband missing. Mrs Garvie phoned him later that same day and said she was convinced her husband would attend a flying club meeting the next night. Later she phoned to say he had not attended the meeting and that she now wished to report him missing.

Mrs Garvie told him that she had not been concerned that morning when she woke up and found her husband gone as she knew he had intended to take the plane to Strathallan that morning and then go to Edinburgh. Later she found her husband's car parked at the hangar. She thought he had taken off in the plane.

On May 16, she went to the airfield and found the plane still in the hangar. She formed the opinion he had arranged to meet someone and they had gone off in one car to Edinburgh.

Sheila Garvie's mother came to the police station on August 16 and gave certain information. She was in a state of collapse; Sergeant Grant called a doctor, who gave her a sedative.

When Peters was charged the next day, he did not try to conceal that he was involved in the murder. He looked ashamed and wanted to get something off his chest. He told the sergeant he wanted to confess but was scared of Tevendale. He said he liked Tevendale as 'a pal' but after what had happened he was scared of him. He said that what happened that night could happen to him too.

Detective-Constable Denis Irvine said he was in a room at the police station with Tevendale on August 16 when Tevendale said: 'Get a car. I will take you to the body at Lauriston.' Tevendale added: 'Let's go. I didn't shoot him but I will tell you about that afterwards.'

He left with other officers and drove under Tevendale's directions. Tevendale indicated where to stop. It was a wild, tangled sort of place. It was very obvious that Tevendale knew exactly where he was going. It was about 5 a.m. He pointed in a certain direction and said: 'He's down there, along that way.' He pointed to an old cycle frame which they removed, finding a shaft two feet square and nine feet deep. There was a tunnel two feet wide and three and a half feet high. Coming from the end of the tunnel was an unpleasant smell; Detective-Constable Irvine assumed a body was there.

Back at the police station, Tevendale made a full statement, in which he said:

I met Maxie Garvie at an SNP outing at Bannockburn. I had a few drinks with him and his wife and was invited flying next day. The following weekend I went to a hotel for drinks with them. The next weekend I was invited to the farm. We went out drinking. After a few drinks I went to bed.

A short time later Sheila was pushed into the room and the door was shut. She said she had been told to spend the night in there or else.

Later that week Sheila came to my work and said Max wanted us to go for a drink that evening. When I arrived, he gave me the car keys and told me to take Sheila out as he was going out with someone else. This happened a few weeks running. On three successive Saturdays we went to Glasgow and Edinburgh, spending the weekend in various hotels.

One night when I was out with Max himself he started making strange advances. At the time I was driving the car and I pulled up at the side of the road and told him that if he did not stop I would belt him. He laughed this off as if it were a joke.

Afterwards we had a few drinks at the farm and I went up to bed. Shortly after he came in and sat on the edge of the bed. He was wearing a dressing gown but was naked underneath. I told him that if he did not leave the room I would get up, dress and go home. He again laughed and left the room.

One Saturday night, after we had been out drinking, he suggested it would be a good idea to toss up to see who slept with

Sheila. Sheila objected and was told to shut up. He tossed the coin and I won. He went through to sleep in the room that I usually had.

About 6 a.m. I woke up and found that he was also lying in the bed. Sheila later told me he had tried to have kinky sex with her when he came in. She refused and he was scared the noise would wake me up. He once told me he loved me more than he loved Sheila.

He often offered me pills of various shapes and sizes which he usually took himself when he was drinking. I once flew with him when we were both severely intoxicated. When we landed he told me he was going to try out a new variation in homo-type sex with Sheila. If she did not like it, he would break her neck.

Matters finally got to a head and Sheila walked out on him. He threatened to shoot her and the kids and me if she did not go back. She did not go back but she was forcibly removed at 3 a.m. the following morning. She went to the doctor to complain about Max's strange sexual ideas and the doctor immediately phoned Max.

When she got home he twisted her arm so far up her back that she had to get the doctor, who was told by Max that she had fallen.

Tevendale then described being set upon in an alley, where he got a slight gash on the face accompanied by the words: 'That's a present from the Skipper.' He assumed it was from Max.

He recalled getting a call from Sheila, who was in a terrible state. She told him Max had come in and was pouring himself a drink, so she went to bed.

She said that a little while later he (Max) came upstairs carrying a rifle and told her that if she did not let him put it up her – he would shoot her. He stripped and got on the bed. There was a grab for the gun and he got shot.

> This is where I come in now. I rolled him up in a sheet and a bit of canvas groundsheet, trailed him downstairs, then put him in the car and drove it. I have missed out a bit about cleaning up. I got a cloth with water and with Sheila cleaned up the mess.

Tevendale then admitted dumping Max's body in the old tunnel, which he knew when he was a boy in the area.

Tevendale's long statement to the police was challenged in court on the grounds that it had been given under undue

presure. After a four-hour debate in the absence of the jury
Lord Thomson ruled it was admissible.

Tevendale did not give evidence in his own defence but he ·
did appear in the witness box during the legal debate to
explain how he came to make the statement. The judge also
examined two policemen before ruling that the statement
should go before the jury. The judge said he was not prepared
to accept Tevendale's allegations of undue pressure, bullying
and physical violence by the police. Tevendale's statement, he
said, could not be said to have been other than spontaneous
and voluntary.

Sheila Garvie, who spent nine hours in the witness box, told
the court her version of the dramatic events that led to the
death of her husband. She and Max had married in 1955 and
had three children, daughters aged 11 and 12 and a son aged
four. Her husband changed about 1962 and began to view sex
'out of all proportion'. She could not cope with the crisis which
arose at that time. She became depressed and went to her
doctor. She was given tranquillisers, but they did not do any
good and later she had consultations with a psychiatrist.

Asked what precipitated the crisis, she said her husband
started to take an interest in nudist clubs and wanted to become
a member. She told him she did not want to become a member
and there was a great argument. Eventually she gave in and he
took her to a nudist club in Edinburgh where there was a small
wooden shed outside a cottage. One nude man insisted on a 12-
year-old girl, also nude, sitting on his knee. Sheila thought it
was disgusting. When they got home she told her husband she
could not go there again.

About this time her husband was taking part in what she
thought was unnatural sexual activity and this upset her very
much. She had to go to a psychiatrist but was too ashamed to
tell him about it. Before that she had never engaged in
perverted or abnormal activity. Although she was pregnant her
husband insisted on taking her and their two daughters to a
naturist camp in Corsica. She had not wanted to go.

Her husband sent away to addresses in London and all kinds
of pornographic pictures and books came back. He had always
been interested in photography and was keen to get her to pose
in the nude. When she protested he said she was inhibited. She

did pose for him one night and learned later that he had shown the photograph to other people. There was nothing indecent about it but she was shocked it had been shown to other people. Her husband seemed to be amused.

Her husband was anxious to form a nudist club of his own and there was an argument about that as well. He went ahead, however, and formed a club in Aberdeenshire, where he took over a cottage. On the day of the opening he wanted her to undress and perform the opening ceremony but she refused.

She described an incident at a party in 1967 at which she found the hostess sitting on her husband's knee. Later she found them together in a bedroom. She was terribly upset and on the way home her husband stopped the car and hit her. She had never seen him like that before.

Max became friendly with Brian and invited him to the farm. He took him flying and they went fishing together.

> When Brian spent weekends with us we had drinks and played records. My husband by this time had taken a great dislike to a brightly-lit room. He had even taken the bulb out of the hall and put darkened bulbs in the sitting room. He brought out candles we used at Christmas and said he liked candlelight.

On one occasion, while they were playing records by candlelight her husband went upstairs, saying he was tired. When she went to bed he asked her intimate questions about Brian which she thought were filthy. It was apparent he took the view that she and Brian had been intimate downstairs but she told him that was not so.

Her husband became friendly with Brian's sister Trudy and on two occasions Sheila lifted the phone and overheard conversations between them. She was terribly upset. At that time she had never been unfaithful.

> I just lost all respect for my husband. I tried to tell my mother about it. My husband bore no resemblance to the man I had known earlier. By the time I turned to my father I had already committed adultery. If I had turned to him earlier he would have helped me.

Her husband encouraged her to be with Brian and eventually she fell in love with him. Max asked her to tell him about her relationship and wanted information of a very intimate and detailed kind. Max suggested she should have intercourse with Brian.

One evening she had a lot to drink and Max was making all sorts of suggestions. Brian went off to bed, leaving them downstairs. When they went upstairs she went to the bathroom; when she came out her husband was standing there very excited. He more or less pushed her into the bedroom with Brian. She stayed the whole night and returned to her own bedroom in the morning. She did not commit adultery with Brian until after her husband's affair with Trudy began.

Her husband had taunted her that he had done things with Trudy that she was not prepared to do. He told her he had given £100 to Brian to entertain her and became very excited by the foursome.

On one occasion when Trudy was not present Max and Brian tossed a coin to see who would sleep with Sheila. On another occasion all three of them shared the same bed. She had never indulged in this kind of thing in her life. There were occasions when she slept with Brian and her husband insisted she return to their room in the morning to make love. She was very ashamed and her health was affected.

She became emotionally involved with Brian but her husband did not want that. At the meeting to try to mend their marriage Max told her she would have to choose between him and Brian and she said she would stay with Brian. She left her husband and saw a lawyer about divorce but then went back to him. By then her husband had finished with Trudy.

Max later suggested her friendship with Brian should be renewed. She was terribly upset about everything and asked Brian to take her away. They went to Bradford but she missed the children. She was terribly distressed and later went to London Airport to meet her husband.

When they got home, Max asked her to describe her intimacies with Brian. On one occasion he held a broken glass at her face, pulled her by the hair and twisted her arm. She was screaming and he threw her against a wall. Her husband's demands had increased. They were unnatural and caused her great distress.

On the night of May 14, she and her husband had a drink,

then had intercourse and fell asleep. She remembered someone pulling at her arms. She was terribly sleepy. Brian took her out of the bedroom and she saw a fair-haired man.

I was dazed and could not think what was happening. I had no idea what Brian was doing there. I heard the most terrible thumping noises. Earlier I noticed Brian was carrying a gun. Afterwards he told me 'He won't worry you any more'. By this time I knew something terrible had happened. I heard something being dragged from the bedroom and being bumped downstairs.

Brian gave her the gun and told her to put it away. Then she heard a car leaving.

I felt morally responsible for what happened because I had allowed Brian to fall in love with me. I felt I had unconsciously provoked him into a state in which he reacted. I took a decision that night that whatever happened I would protect Brian because he had done this for me. I had reached a crossroads in my life.

She sat up all night and at dawn Brian phoned to say he had left a package of Max's clothes in the garage. She put them in a wardrobe and saw that the mattress was saturated in blood.

But she denied telling Trudy Birse anything to indicate she had a hand in her husband's killing. The only part she played was in concealing the fact he was dead. She did not know how long she would have to live with her secret. At no time was she ever going to betray Brian. She would commit suicide rather than betray him. Her life then became a course of deception and she felt a broken woman with no self-respect whatever.

Asked why she continued her association with Tevendale in the knowledge of how her husband was killed, she said: 'I was, and still am, in love with Brian and I wanted to protect him. He did it to protect me. I felt I could not betray him.'

Cross-examined, she said she willingly went on the foursomes and enjoyed being with Brian. Life became unbearable but she was prepared to put up with it for the sake of the children.

After her husband's death, she admitted before the court, she met Brian three times a week and they made love. She shared the bed of the man whom she knew had murdered her husband but she was not a party to the murder. Brian had spoken of beating up her husband and said he deserved it but she did not know he was going to kill him.

Peters told the court a third version of the events that took place on the night of May 14. He said he wanted to go to the police to get it off his chest but he would have been frightened for the rest of his life if he gave Tevendale away.

Tevendale had asked him to drive that night and Mrs Garvie let them into the house. She did not look surprised. In the sitting room Brian loaded a gun with bullets from his pocket. He felt it was rather strange he should load a gun. 'I was scared. I didn't know what he was going to use the gun for. I was afraid.'

Mrs Garvie gave them drinks and showed them to a room upstairs. She left them in the room with the light out. Brian told him to keep quiet and say nothing. Fifteen minutes later Mrs Garvie came back and said, 'He's asleep now.' Brian said to follow him and they went into a bedroom where there was a man asleep. Brian struck the man several times on the back of the head with the butt of the rifle, then picked up a pillow and put it on his head, then shot him through the pillow. There was only one shot. Mrs Garvie was outside the room.

'I didn't say anything. I was horrified. I felt sick.'

Brian produced a groundsheet from a rucksack he had brought and they wrapped the body in it. Peters felt if he did not help he would get the same.

They took the body to the garage. Then Brian and Mrs Garvie went to make coffee. He did not feel like drinking the coffee. They put the body in the back seat of his car and Brian told him to follow him. They each drove to the airfield, where Brian got in his car and gave him directions. When they arrived at the entrance to a tunnel, Brian went down a hole and told him to push the body down. They dragged it along the tunnel and covered it with stones.

He was not trying to implicate Mrs Garvie but she was there and met them at the door. Peters strenuously denied he played any part in the killing of Max Garvie. He did not know what was going to happen. He was afraid of Tevendale and the gun. He denied that he knew quite well what was going to happen.

Asked what he got for it all Peters replied, 'I never got

nothing, nothing at all.' But he agreed that afterwards Brian and Mrs Garvie looked after him well. His wedding reception was at Mrs Birse's house and he got a wedding present of £5 from Mrs Garvie and an electric heater from Brian and Mrs Garvie.

Mr Ewan Stewart told the jury of the part Mrs Garvie played in Peters' wedding. She provided and cooked the turkey and also provided the wine. If she was innocent was it remotely conceivable that she would start to have such dealings with a youth she said she had not seen until the night of her husband's death? Could she have felt anything but revulsion for the assistant murderer? The only conclusion could be that there was some bond between these three people.

Mrs Garvie had painted herself after the murder as a broken woman suffering anxiety and unhappiness and contemplating suicide but there were photographs showing her and Tevendale at picnics before their arrest. Mr Stewart passed the photographs to the jurors and asked them to decide whether she looked like 'a broken woman'. They also knew that by this time she was sleeping three nights a week with Tevendale while her mother looked after the children.

Mr Stewart summed up Tevendale's explanation as 'a quite impossible fabrication'. Tevendale had a strong motive for murder and had been uttering threats about Max Garvie. Mrs Birse had got what was virtually a confession of murder from Tevendale and Mrs Garvie and when the final day of reckoning came Tevendale took the police to the body.

Peters, he said, had played an essential part in the murder plan. There was one damning fact against him. He told the police that Tevendale said he was wanting to get rid of a bloke and would he go with him so that he could have transport. Peters had a peculiar defence of coercion but what had been established was not consistent with such a defence. Peters was not forced to do anything at gunpoint.

Dealing with Mrs Garvie's part, he asked, 'Was she the real brain behind this crime?' She had everything to gain by its successful completion. She would get rid of a husband with whom she said life was hell and would be free to entertain her lover while continuing the life to which she had become accustomed.'

Mr Stewart said that while he was not suggesting that money was the motive it was right the jury should know Sheila Garvie stood to gain a fortune by her husband's death. She was a resourceful woman and, on her own admission, a skilled liar. She must be 'as hard as nails' to do what she had done.

Tevendale must have entered the house knowing she was passively cooperative. Why no screams? Why no action to save her husband? After the murder she helped the murderers conceal and destroy evidence. It was a deliberately planned murder executed with care, Mr Stewart said.

Dr Taylor, for Peters, said his client was no more guilty of the murder than a taxi driver would have been. He did not assist in the murder and did not try to interfere because he was afraid that if he did he would 'get it'.

Referring to Tevendale telling his sister that Peters struck Max Garvie with an iron bar, Dr Taylor said Tevendale knew his sister was fond of Max and he told her the murder had occurred in this way so that he himself would not be made out to be too much of a monster.

Peters' wedding reception at the Birse house was a very strange and macabre situation, given that everyone present, with the exception of Peters' wife, knew Max Garvie had been murdered. 'Were they watching Peters? Did they realise he was the weak link and that they had to keep him in sight? I ask you to accept that Peters did not know he was driving Tevendale to murder. His assistance in disposing of the body is not murder. There is no accessory after the fact in murder in Scotland. Alan Peters is an honest lad. He is not like the others. He is the fly drawn into the spider's web and I submit he is innocent.'

Mr Daiches, for Sheila Garvie, told the jury that while a great deal of sensational evidence had been presented in the case, he intended to tear to shreds the web in which the Crown sought to enmesh Mrs Garvie. If, in doing so, he ranged from Balmoral to the beaches of Corsica it was in the interests of justice.

> This brilliant young man with everything that life could afford, a beautiful wife, a lovely home and three children, all the money in the world, surrounded by friends and admirers . . . everything that the heart of man could desire. Something stopped it and he

degenerated. He started some kind of personality change. That change set in motion a chain of events which increased in intensity and dramatic content until they reached the night of the 14th–15th May.

No one had suggested, Mr Daiches said, that before the change in her husband Sheila Garvie was a flirt, let alone an adultress. She was a happy wife, a good mother.

This indeed was the tragedy — that step by step this degenerative process took place. And step by step, powerless to resist, Maxwell and Sheila Garvie were propelled to the edge of the abyss descending to the Valley of Shadows — he to his death and she to the dock charged with his murder.

Sheila Garvie had to be conditioned over a period of time to accept this kind of activity that Max demanded. In this her husband was only too successful, but what he did not appreciate when he pushed her into the arms of Tevendale was that they would become emotionally involved. He brought the young man from a different stratum of society, gave him money, wined and dined him and took him to hotels where he could not otherwise afford to go.

'It resulted in Sheila and Tevendale falling in love. This was almost like Lady Chatterley with a tragic ending having regard to the differences in ages and social background of these two people. It was easy for Max to give up Trudy, for she had been nothing to him but a convenience.'

Mr Daiches also argued that if Sheila Garvie had done the 'Lady Macbeth' act and let in the murderers, she would have wanted to know that the place of concealment was a place forever secure.

Mr Cameron, for Tevendale, said there was no evidence that his client had shown malice or ill-will towards Max Garvie before the night of 14th–15th May. On the evidence, the indictment against him should be found not proven.

Spectators queued from 3 a.m. to get seats for the final day of the trial on 2 December 1968. The jury did not waste any time and returned an hour later with their verdict.

They found Sheila Garvie guilty by a majority and her bearded lover, Brian Tevendale, guilty unanimously. Both were sentenced to life imprisonment.

By a majority, they found the charges against Peters not proven and he was discharged from the dock.

Lord Thomson said it had been a long, tiring, difficult and, in some respects, very sordid case. The jury had heard a great deal of evidence relating to peculiarities of sexual behaviour and to sexual perversion. It had been said that Max Garvie was a sexual pervert who forced his perversion on his wife but it was just as wrong to kill such a man as to kill a man who was sexually normal.

There had been a picture painted in court of a quartet who had a pattern of sexual relationships and activity that the jury might regard as nauseating and falling below even the conventional standards of the so-called permissive society. It was not a question of whether the persons concerned were moral, immoral or amoral but whether each of them was guilty of murder.

There was a hostile demonstration outside the court as Trudy Birse and her husband left the building. Several hundred people gathered and booed and jeered them. The crowd spilled over from the pavement on to the road outside, blocking the traffic. The Birses took refuge in a nearby office for an hour; then the police cleared the way as they fled in a taxi.

Neither Sheila Garvie nor Tevendale lodged appeals against the jury's verdicts and both served long sentences before eventually being released.

Many of Max Garvie's closest friends and colleagues were incensed by the picture of him painted by the witnesses in court and they took out an advertisement to defend his good name.

The person they had heard described in court was not the Max Garvie they knew. But while some of the allegations about him may well have been exaggerated, there was enough independent evidence to show that he was a complex man who changed from a happy carefree husband to a man obsessed with sex.

CHAPTER 10
The Gambling Chinese Waiter

Both fact and fiction in the United States have given a new meaning to the word 'contract' but the offering of a sum of money to someone for his services as a murderer is a very rare event indeed in this country.

Yet, in 1984, rumours swept the city of Edinburgh that the father of a teenage disco manageress who was found strangled, suspended from a spiral staircase, had put out a contract for £30,000 on the life of a gambling Chinese waiter who was in prison awaiting trial for her murder.

When the father, 60-year-old John 'Paddy' Reilly, gave evidence in the High Court in Edinburgh in October of that year he strongly denied the rumour about such a contract as 'complete and utter nonsense'. All he had offered was a £5,000 reward for information leading to the conviction of his daughter's killer. But the rumour persisted, reaching Saughton Prison, where 26-year-old Shu-Kee Leung, a native of Hong Kong, was being held. Leung became so terrified he would be killed that he volunteered to go before a local sheriff and gave his version of events in the disco office in the late afternoon of April 27.

Leung told the sheriff a bizarre story of how he was forced by two gangsters at gunpoint to hang Pauline Reilly's body on the staircase when she was already dead. He said he decided to tell the truth because he was in fear for his life, both because of these gangsters and because of the contract he had heard about in prison.

The brutal and callous murder of pretty 19-year-old Pauline Reilly in Annabel's Disco in Fountainbridge, Edinburgh, where she was part-owner and worked as a day manageress, proved to be a most complex and unusual case, testing the skills of the police forensic science team to the limit as they painstakingly uncovered evidence damning to Leung.

Police faced a daunting task when they arrived on the scene of the murder. The disco office was full of papers, diaries, ledgers, and records of names, addresses and phone numbers. They even had to empty the waste paper basket and piece together every scrap of paper like pieces in a jigsaw.

The motive for the murder at least seemed clear, as the heavy doors of the wall safe hung open. Till rolls and other records showed that about £3,100 was missing.

Forensic scientists began to reconstruct the crime. It appeared the girl was attacked at her desk and strangled. Then her body was hung from a spiral staircase.

The police uncovered two crucial clues. On the floor by Pauline's desk they found a knife; beside her chair, a piece of paper with Leung's name, address and telephone number scrawled on it. The name meant nothing to the investigators at the time; it was just one of hundreds of names and addresses in the office.

Leung was interviewed as a matter of course but denied any knowledge of the crime and claimed the handwriting was not his. He suggested that his estranged wife might have written down his name and address some months earlier when she worked in the disco as a barmaid.

But the police were more immediately successful with the knife. They traced the manufacturer, discovering that they had sent a consignment to Ladbrokes for their Edinburgh hotel, the Dragonara. There, the knives were used only in the Terrace Restaurant, where Leung was a waiter.

Attention then centred on the piece of paper with Leung's name and address on it. Forensic tests showed indentations from the previous page on a notepad. These matched another piece of the notepad with cash figures which Pauline Reilly had been working on the day she was killed.

If the address was indeed in Leung's handwriting then it placed him in the office on the day Pauline had died. Leung was arrested and provided samples of his handwriting which, despite his attempt to disguise it, was later proved to be identical to that on the piece of paper. Part of a fingerprint found on the piece of paper was also found to be Leung's, thus completing the jigsaw.

But more evidence against Leung was to be uncovered. When police searched his battered Lancia they found £2,200 hidden in the spare wheel cover and another £260 under the handbrake mounting. Scientists also found from microscopic examination of Leung's clothing that fibres on his jacket were identical to those of the jumper the dead girl was wearing. There were also fibres on her jumper matching those from Leung's jacket.

At his trial, Leung at first denied any involvement but later claimed he had been implicated by two gangsters to whom he owed a gambling debt. Leung denied threatening the girl with a knife, seizing hold of her, placing a ligature round her throat and strangling her. He also denied robbing her of £3,123 and stealing a knife from the Dragonara Hotel.

The dead girl's father wept in court as he described finding her body at 6.40 p.m. when he arrived to re-stock the bar. At first he thought it was his 22-year-old daughter, Dawn, who was joint owner of the disco with Pauline. It was only when Dawn arrived at the disco that he realised it was Pauline's body. He had seen her at lunchtime that day when he went to the office to sign pay cheques. Her dog was with her at that time. He had warned her in the past not to work in the office with the safe open.

The dead girl's aunt, Miss Margaret Reilly, said she had done some cleaning at the disco and left at 3.25 p.m. that day. Pauline had said she would be home at 4.30 p.m. but she failed to appear.

Pathologist Dr Anthony Busuttil said the girl was strangled with a rope wound three times round her neck and was left suspended from the spiral staircase. A sash cord had been applied from behind while the girl was standing and she would have fallen unconscious within seconds of the rope being pulled tight. There were no signs of a struggle. The same ligature was used to strangle her as to suspend her body from the staircase. She would be dead or almost dead by the time she was strung up on the staircase.

The dead girl's sister, Dawn, said Mrs Leung had worked as a barmaid at the disco for three or four months. She had met Leung himself when he called at the disco in August 1983 to ask her to dismiss his wife. His marriage was on the rocks and his wife working until 3 a.m. was making things worse, he told her. She replied it was none of her concern. She saw him in the disco several times after that.

Leung's estranged wife, Norah, was called to give evidence but when the judge, Lord Robertson, told her she need not give evidence against her husband, she said she would rather not and left the witness box.

Ahmed Lahmamsi, another waiter at the Dragonara Hotel who worked with Leung, told the court that before he was arrested Leung told him he had won £2,000 at a gambling casino.

'He was very excited about winning the money and when I said I did not believe it he showed me some of the money.'

Robert Taylor, the manager of the Royal Chimes Casino in Royal Terrace, Edinburgh, said Leung was a regular gambler and had called three of four times a week for the last three years. His staff, he said, were on the lookout for people wishing to 'launder' money but they would become suspicious only when strangers came in with large sums of money.

Money could be 'laundered' by changing cash into chips and then later cashing the chips for exactly the same amount of money, leaving the 'hot' money in the casino.

A member of the staff at the casino recalled cashing in chips for £2,000 in £100 notes for Leung at the beginning of May 1984, shortly after the murder.

A restaurant waiter, Eric Raymbaut, said that two days after the murder he saw Leung in the casino. He was attracted by the size and type of bets Leung was placing. He was betting £200 a time in cash in the boxes on the roulette table covering a dozen numbers. It was unusual for stakes to be so high backing 'dozens'. In his experience normally bets would be about £10 or £20. He saw Leung place 10 or 12 bets in cash and others using chips.

Dominic Bate, who had worked with Leung at the Caledonian Hotel, Edinburgh, said Leung came to stay with his family after separating from his wife. He understood Leung was in trouble financially and he believed he had debts of around £1,000. He himself had loaned Leung a sum of money and part of it was repaid before Leung's arrest. Leung still owed him £120.

Several witnesses saw Leung in the vicinity of the disco on the afternoon of the murder.

Anne Donoghue said she saw him about 4.20 p.m. She spoke

to him for a few minutes and then he said he was on his way to work. Leung had owed the company she worked for more than £1,500 but he had repaid all but £632 of it. During their conversation that day he said he would call the following week. On May 4 he paid a further £100 towards his debt.

The head waiter at the Caledonian Hotel saw Leung walking down Lothian Road near the disco about 4.30 p.m. Witnesses also spoke of seeing two foreign-looking men near the doorway of the disco. One of them was described as looking like Libyan leader Colonel Ghadaffi.

Detective Chief Inspector Norman Deland, who had only just retired from the police identification branch, was asked by Mr Donald Macaulay, QC (now Lord Macaulay of Bragar), who represented Leung, how many times in his service he had known an alleged murderer to leave his name and address and, as it transpired, a fingerprint, lying in the same place as the body. The detective said he could only recall this happening once in his 28 years as a policeman. Another detective told the court it was unique in his experience.

Inspector Deland said he asked Leung to provide specimens of his handwriting and asked him to write down the same name and address as was on the piece of paper. As he was doing so Leung became quite agitated. After watching one or two examples of Leung's handwriting Deland formed quite a definite opinion that Leung was trying to disguise his writing.

Mr Deland, a handwriting and fingerprint expert, said he had reached the view that the writing on the piece of paper and on the specimens by Leung were by the same author. He also found an impression on the piece of paper of Leung's left forefinger.

Leung told the court that three days before his trial he made a declaration to a sheriff alleging the girl was already dead when he arrived at the disco and that he was forced by gangsters to hang up the body. In his statement, the court was told, Leung said he met a man called Hasin in a casino in late March or early April. He lost all his money and Hasin gave him £10. A week later he saw Hasin again in the casino and Hasin gave him another £50. He later repaid £40.

On the afternoon of the murder Hasin phoned asking for the balance of £20. He told him to meet him outside a cinema near the disco. When Hasin arrived, Leung said, he gave him the money. Then they went to the disco because Hasin said he had left his car keys there. The door was opened by a man in a white tee-shirt.

'When I got in I saw a young girl lying in the middle of the room and I see this guy walk to the corner near the windows. He was putting a pair of white gloves on. I was really shocked and did not know what to do.'

Leung said he asked them, 'What happened to the girl?' and they told him, 'We killed her and that's what we do for a living.'

They told him they wanted to get him involved and to be one of them in the future. They said it was easy work with lots of money. He told them he wanted to go and that he would not tell anyone but the man in the tee-shirt said, 'You don't think we would let you go just like that.'

The man in the tee-shirt produced a gun and said they knew where his wife and child lived. He was told if he did not do as he was told he would have his head blown off. He was told to write down his name and address and he did so. He was then told to move the body to the stairs and to tie it up.

'I was that frightened. I can't even think why they wanted me to hang her up for she is dead already. It doesn't make sense at all. But I just wanted to get out . . . to get it over with.'

As he did this he was photographed as 'just a little guarantee'. The man gave him £200 and a bag of coins ad he had no other choice but to take them. After they left the disco, Hasin and a third man, the driver of a nearby parked car, took him to work at the hotel.

The next day Hasin phoned and Leung was taken to a flat in Tollcross where the man with the tee-shirt said that a knife from Leung's hotel and a piece of paper with his name and address on it had been left in the disco office. He asked them if they were putting the blame on him and was told that it would be enough to get the attention of the police and give them time to get away.

Leung told the sheriff he decided to tell because he was arrested and they were still free. They were gangsters and would do anything they thought was necessary. The dead girl's father thought he was one of the gang and had put out a £30,000 reward to kill him.

Leung, in evidence, said the man in the tee-shirt was British and had a Liverpool accent. When he was taken to the disco the girl was already dead. Her face was 'black and purple', he said.

He told the jury if he was cleared of the murder and robbery he would have to flee the country because he feared he would be killed by the gangsters who had murdered and robbed the girl. They would stop at nothing, he said, now that he had told the truth about them. He had decided to tell the whole truth when he heard in prison that Pauline's father had put out a 'contract' for £30,000 on his life. He agreed he had lied to the police and a sheriff in his first statement. He did so out of fear because he was warned he should not mention certain people in connection with Pauline Reilly. Although he was in the disco the day she died he had taken no part in her death.

'I swear to God I did not kill her and I did not steal the money.'

Asked by Mr Donald Mackay, prosecuting, why he was 'singled out' by these men to take the blame for the murder and robbery, he said it must be because he was a well-known gambler at the Royal Chimes Casino. A few days before the murder, he claimed, he had winnings of between £3,000 and £4,000. He put some of his winnings in his car because he thought it was the safest place. He had gone back to the casino after the murder hoping to find Hasin or the other man but had failed to trace them.

He denied the prosecution's suggestion that he had made up his second story involving the two men because he realised forensic evidence had proved conclusively that he had been in the disco that day.

That indeed was the crux of the matter, for it was after the defence became aware of the convincing forensic evidence placing him in the disco that day that Leung produced his fantastic tale.

The jury found Leung guilty of murder and robbery by a majority at the end of the seven-day trial. The court was told that Leung, who had come from Hong Kong in 1975, had minor previous convictions and was on deferred sentence for theft at the time of the murder. Lord Robertson said he had no alternative but to send him to prison for life.

A few months later, three judges in the Court of Criminal

Appeal rejected Leung's appeal against his conviction. They said the case against him was strong and that the jury's verdict could not be described as perverse.

In his appeal, Leung attempted to draw attention to 'bizarre and unexplained aspects' of his case, but Lord Justice General Emslie said these issues had all been considered by the jury in reaching their majority verdict.

Mr Reilly said his daughter's death was all so senseless. Leung could have taken the money and left her alone. He probably intended tying her up but something went terribly wrong and he panicked. Reilly thought his daughter was far too trusting. He had warned her to be careful but she would open the door to anyone.

But several riddles about the crime remain unanswered. Why was Leung so stupid as to leave two obvious 'calling cards' behind — the knife, which could be traced to the hotel where he worked, and a note with his name and address on it? And why was it necessary to kill the teenage girl just for the sake of £3,100? The third mystery was why she was left tied to the spiral staircase when she was already dead.

The police theory at the time seemed the likeliest explanation. They believed Leung, desperate for money, knew the layout and pattern of work at the disco. He went there with robbery in mind and pretended he wanted to make a booking.

His English was not very good and Pauline probably asked him to write down his name and address and telephone number on a sheet of paper from her notepad. Then Leung produced the knife and threatened her with it. He was probably forced to kill her when he realised she recognised him. In his panic to get away with the cash, he forgot all about the incriminating note and the knife. But why he tied her body to the spiral staircase will probably never be known.